A Curious Poet

The Work of a Year

for the friends and the strangers I meet in the street

for the people I love who love me too

for the artists and jokers who make my life sweet

the work of my life is for you

Other Books

A Sudden Poet

The Great Life and Other Stories

Last year, in Spring, something changed, and I began to write; poetry, mostly, and the odd piece of prose. My writing is sacred and satirical, vulgar and sweet. I am humoured by old-fashioned language, and my fancy is much tickled by form. I write about God, nature, death, politics, Devizes, love, trees, friends, shopping, trolls, and angels. I like a nice sonnet, me, a cheeky tanka, a mischievous couplet, and the sheer exhilaration of an alternate rhyme scheme. I've responded to the wisdom and foolishness of the world with soft and angry words. Inspiration has come from strange places, from unusual people and odd muses, from the cyber shadows and on the altar step. I have laid my faith bare in 'The Curious Offering of the Sacristan', and written the pure filth of 'The Vengeance of Rhyming Mary'.

My work reaches from the gutter to the sky and down again. Come for the ride.

This is the work of a year.

© Gail Foster 2016

Works are arranged chronologically within chapters, with the earliest first.
After much agonising over the issue of bad language I decided to leave it all in. You have been warned.
The more sensitive reader may wish to avoid some of the rhymes in 'Faffing About On Facebook', and 'The Vengeance of Rhyming Mary' in 'Fair Game'.

Index

Death and Epitaphs (16)

Faffing About On Facebook (21)

Told You So (13)

With Love (21)

Two Short Stories

Other Things (17)

Christians, Druids, and Light (19)

Fair Game

Election Dis Function

Tin Pot Dictator; *written for the Devizes Festival Poetry Slam*

Out of Line

Performance Poetry; *Open Mic at The Bear*

Fair Game; *hunting isn't tennis*

Swine and Pearls

Spot On, Harry; *Harry Styles from One Direction corrects a fan's punctuation at a gig*

Corbyn's Labour

Corbyn's Muses

Jihadi John; a Clerihew

Trump Flowers; *to be sung to the tune of 'Nelly the Elephant'*

Katie Hopkins; Wild Redemption

Satire and the Soul

Baby Talk

The Wobbly Bog; *regarding an unwanted water feature*

My Arse; a Lament

The Vengeance of Rhyming Mary; *a reply to an obscene suggestion somewhat offensive to poets*

Election Dis Function

The parties are all over
Fat smug ladies have sung
Today we know our Parliament
Is not Well Hung

A loud triumphal snort was heard
As Georgie passed the line
We've got a Tory Government
And the rich will do just fine

Corks have been popping
Lemons have been sucked
We've got us a new Parliament
And the poor are F*cked

Farewell to the old guard
Their ghostly voices haunt the halls
Now there's a new Government
That's got no Balls

In the graveyard there's an Edstone
Under which Nick sleeps uneasy
We've got us a new Parliament
And Farage is feeling queasy

Now we'll all be shafted
By old Etonians and bankers
We've got a right wing Government
You put them there, you wankers

Hoorah for the posh boys
Break out the champagne and the coke
You voted in the Tories!
What a f*cking joke

Tin Pot Dictator

You're a Tin Pot Dictator, you're Kim Jong Un
Blasting me to pieces with an anti-aircraft gun
For momentary guard slip and forgetting of pretence
Public execution for your Minister of Defence

There were less dramatic options, like demotion and sacking
Not as entertaining, mind, as death by ack-acking
As for that piss take poster in the Ealing barber's shop
You'd show them a Bad Hair Day with a more severe crop

You're a Tin Pot Dictator, you're that bloke Pol Pot
Who tried to turn the clock back to Year Zero, or Dot
It must have been torture, being rubbish at school
So you got rid of all the clever ones that made you feel a fool

Clad with a well cut uniform and medals on your chest
A gun, a throne and megaphone you're better than the rest
Making up for all those failings that you feel so acutely
Power that tendeth to corrupt, in you corrupteth absolutely

You're a Tin Pot Dictator, going by the name of Vlad
As in Lenin and Putin and that weird Impaler lad
You're Saddam Hussein and you're Ho Chi Minh
Declare resistance to be futile and dissent a sin

Flatter your enemies lest they stab you in the back
Equip the walls with ears to hear what loyalty you lack
Hide the Stasi in the khasi to hear the shit go down
Watch for subtle facial movements like the nuance of a frown

You're a Tin Pot Dictator, but Godwins Law states
That the first to mention Hitler loses rational debates
From bad art and rejection came forth carnage we presume
Stick a moustache on the elephant in the middle of the room

Rally troops remaining, keep the enemy at the gate
For there just might be a coup, and it just might be too late
There are movements in the corners of the bunker in your mind
Where one eye is always open in the kingdom of the blind

You're a Tin Pot Dictator, mowing down the picket
You're the warden who gave a crate of vegetables a ticket
Break out the tar and feathers if I ever call you mate
I am the voice of decompression in a tin pot state

Out of Line

"Order, order!" he shouted "We're all out of line"

"I'll see to that" quoth the whore

"And if you're a good boy we'll do three in a bed,

You can snort off my titties and more"

Oh silly old Sewel you poor addled old fool

So clearly misguided and randy

That the question of cash and the secretive flash

Were obscured in a cloud of nose candy

Performance Poetry

Mad gladiator
Tossing herself to lions
Armed with only wit

Disinhibited
Titties brought out for the lads
In verbal foreplay

Lyrical satire
Like pencils sharped for pricking
Holes in lead balloons

From naughty corner
More by wine amused than rhyme
A shadow giggles

The tumbleweed blows
Words settle on silent ground
With one hand clapping

The poet's cloak hides
Shoulders warm and broad enough
To quiver with mirth

Fair Game

Tally ho boys, sound the horn
The fox is on the run
Who let the dogs out
On a killing spree for fun
Tally ho boys, we're entitled
We few, we happy band
To terrorise your wildlife
As we trample on your land

From the hedge a wordsmith
Chuckles with defiance
Cropping out the 'orsie'
From the '**Countryside**alliance'

Swine and Pearls

Snuffling for truffles

Scenting morsels of delight

Delirious swine

Drowning in the oyster beds

Drunk on mysterious wine

Spot On, Harry

Harry Styles is really great
He knows how to punctuate
And he learnt to spell at school
Harry, man, you're really cool
Better read than Harry Potter
A rarer breed, a comma spotter
Tell us, Harry, in your pop
What's the point of a full stop?

Corbyn's Labour

From something old

Comes something new

A different shade

More red than blue

From Old Labour

Borrowing

Good favour

And

A following

Corbyn's Muses

Don't call us Babes, such nonsense just confuses

We're equals standing side by side with men

If you must, then coin us Corbyn's Muses

Inspiring hearts and minds with voice and pen

We've got here through integrity and toil

Intelligence and knowledge of the game

We'll labour endlessly for British soil

Don't denigrate us with a silly name

Jihadi John; a clerihew

So farewell to the Scouse Jihadi

God knows what the bloke was on

What evil scum, a proper baddy

F*ck right off Jihadi John

Trump Flowers

With dismay
We watch as he has his say
This is the man who would spurn the Koran
And send all the Muslims away

One dark knight
Who makes his intentions plain
Force Mexicans all to build up a wall
So they'll never be seen again

On telly the hierophant Donald Trump
Is ringmaster of his own circus
On and on like a trumpety skunk
Trump, Trump, Trump...

Donald the hierophant set off a trump
That stank out the political jungle
Blundering on like a trumpety chump
Trump, Chump, Trump

Off-white white, is the colour he has planned
For painting the stage for his mad charade
Across the American land

What new trick is he going to perform
How bad can it get? We've ain't seen nothing yet
But the bonfires are awfully warm

The arrogant turd is appalling
Not far enough away
So wrong on the Right
With a haircut like shite
Followed through-out
The USA...

Oh...

On telly the hierophant Donald Trump
Is ringmaster of his own circus
On and on, like a trumpety skunk
Trump, Trump, Trump...

Donald the hierophant set off a trump
That stank out the political jungle
Blundering on like a trumpety chump
Trump, Trump, Trump...

Katie Hopkins; Wild Redemption

Katie Hopkins, what a bitch

She really makes my innards itch

She's paid to spit and vent her bile

Her views are simply crass and vile

The woman thinks that refugees

Should all die screaming in the seas

And now she is an educator?

Well, Brunel students sure don't rate her

Poor Katie got no praise or thanks

Just fifty silent backs in ranks

Her thoughts upon the welfare state

Perceived to be just tosh and hate

They sent her straight to Coventry

A damned good place for her to be

She's blaming social media

For everyone is wrong but her

Not like she's a cow at all

Or cares if pride precedes a fall

As long as she still earns a wad

She'll carry on like some bad God

Dispensing poison, spitting blood

Dragging free speech through the mud

In years gone by our ears would twitch

A mob would rise and kill the witch

But that was then, and this is now

Best to simply shun the cow

For centuries of love and learning

Persuade us Katie's not for burning

She's bound to go too far one day

For Karma's not a bitch to play

Eternal justice, endless fall

Oh, Katie won't like that at all

Forever with the evil dead, and

Haunted, by the things she's said

Do you really want that, Kate?

It's not too late to recreate

In love there's simply no exemption

Just endless joy and wild redemption...

Satire and The Soul

With satire comes responsibility

Thus spake the bard, regarding cosmic law

'Tis true that thought and act and speech are free

But heed the truth learned by the bards of yore

What goes around and round will soon return

To that dark human place where it began

And pain shall be the lesson he shall learn

Who points his pen in anger at a man

Lest he forget, we none of us shine bright

That are not sullied by some silent shade

And he who seeks another man to slight

May curse the pen that bore the words he made

For what we see in others, we have known

Some simple human neediness or greed

The weakness we perceive is like our own

Who knows a tree that has not seen a seed

So satirise yourself, so spake the bard

Before you dare another man to mock

And turn upon yourself a light as hard

As that with which you wish a man to shock

Unshadow your shortcomings, write them true

Or fall upon your failings like a sword

For this is what you would to others do

And thine own self hast thine own pen ignored

Now weigh the pain you draw like blood from light

With cut of blade, of swift and vicious pen

Look down upon yourself from lofty height

As you would fain look down on other men

What do you see, but merely flesh and fear

A naked frightened soul that cries for love

All sorrow bound and clothed in darkness drear

With eyes up turned in hope to light above

Have pity, spake the bard, for every word
You wield will have the power to wound or heal
Remember what you here have seen and heard
Think twice before you cause a man to feel
The lacerations of your jagged wit
The schadenfreude of your savage ire
Lest you be made to join him in the pit
Lest you be so consumed in that same fire
He snuffed the candle flame, picked up his book
And left the poet, wise from sorrow shown
An unveiled mirror's face in which to look
At imperfection that was his alone

With satire comes responsibility
For what goes forth returns, of that be sure
And you are that which you in others see
The naked frightened soul the poet saw

Baby Talk

Isn't he lovely? the old woman said

And doesn't he look the spit of his Dad

Is he on solids, how long does he sleep

And how many other kids have you had?

Who does he look like? the young woman said

I'm not really sure if he's anyone's kid

I feed him on burgers, he doesn't sleep much

And I've had one for each of the blokes that I did

Not quite the answers the old woman sought

The one about blokes pretty much struck her dumb

The young woman giggled, she'd made it all up

And what's more she wasn't even 'his' Mum

But what fun to be had as she walked around town

To the 'ooohs' and the 'aaahs' and the helium cries

Oh, the amusement of dressing a girl

In an outfit as blue as conventional skies

His name's Rupert, she'd say, (sometimes Nobby or Fred)

Depending on who was that nosey that day

He's got rickets, or measles, whatever disease

Occurred to her, and that seemed funny to say

It entertained baby, she really was bright

And sick of inane inappropriate chat

And of people who leaned far too near to her face

Who were nosey and smelly and frequently spat

She was in on the joke, and well up for the crack

For the stuff folk came out with was simply absurd

She was practising swearwords at night in her cot

To prepare for the day she could utter a word

And then she would show 'em, she'd show 'em alright

Not to treat her as though she was some kind of fool

It's my business how many nappies I fill

Such personal questions, completely uncool

In the meantime, she's watching, she's mentally noting

How humans make speech in particular forms

Who is good, who is bad, who speaks some kind of sense

And who is averse to conventional norms

Oh, babies are little and can't answer back

But don't think for a moment they're not on the ball

They're not poodles, or Martians, or mentally ill

So speak to them nicely, or don't speak at all

The Tale of the Wobbly Bog

Water, water, everywhere
In rushing rivers down the wall
As loud as grand Niagara's Fall
In to the Wobbly Bog

Pouring, pouring, endlessly
Insistent flow of running stream
Unwanted runnels carved through dream
Swelling the Wobbly Bog

Soaking, soaking, soggily
The puddle deep, the muddy ground
'Tis said there was a postman found
Drowned in the Wobbly Bog

Dropping, dropping, gravity
Bleaching brick with scale of lime
On damp of wall the mark of time
Shadows the Wobbly Bog

Gushing, gushing, noisily
Unbalancing the Feng and Shui
No wind to dry the churning sea
Flooding the Wobbly Bog

Madness, madness, sanity
By white noise of incessant drip
Is sunken like a sodden ship
Wrecked in the Wobbly Bog

Misty, misty, spookily
By moonlight come the boggy sprites
With mischief and their tiny lights
Haunting the Wobbly Bog

Wishing, wishing, hopelessly
That some good knight with tool or sword
The landlord, or the Water Board
Might conquer the Wobbly Bog

Watching, watching, grumpily
The paint that never dries; dismay
As Wiltshire waters pour away
In to the Wobbly Bog

My Arse; a Lament

I understand that getting old
Is just a stage we pass
But can anybody tell me
What happened to my arse?

It used to be quite lively
And a distance from the ground
Ashamed to say it though I am
It used to get around

It was nifty on the dance floor
And comfy on a chair
It was pert and it was bouncy
But now there's nothing there

And what is there is saggy
And not worthy of remark
Not flattered much by moonlight
Disappointing in the dark

Inevitable, gravity
That's what it's all about
In some tired hotel lobby
My butt is checking out

Play a mournful serenade
Sound the final horn
'Tis off, my sorry arse, beyond
The Tropic of Capricorn

If I'd have seen it leaving
I could have waved goodbye
Packed a flask and sandwich box
And had a little cry

Ageing, such a pantomime
A farce, a silly plot
"It's behind you!" Not my arse it ain't
It was, but now is not

So, don't take your arse for granted

It's for fun, and sitting on

Enjoy it while you've got one

'Cos you'll miss it when it's gone

The Vengeance of Rhyming Mary

A man whose intellect was dimming
Developed a penchant for rimming
And wrote in to a seedy sonnet
His member, with a poet on it
And as he wrote, things came to pass
Came flying from the poet's ass
Complicated unknown words
Satire, lavender, and turds
Savage metaphor and art
And laughter, blown out with a fart

Not quite the kick he had expected
For which he had his post erected
He beat his meat, he tugged and tossed
But somehow all the power was lost
A flash! A bang! A funny smell!
As Rhyming Mary cast her spell
Dark curses wove from that and this
On he who chose to take the piss
Such vengeance shall the foolish find
Who takes a poet from behind

When all is done, the rhyme complete
There, 'mongst the roses at her feet
A fairy with a tiny cock
Wanking in an ankle sock

Down in The Vize

Computing Rhythm; *The Computers play the Corn Exchange*

Whasson, You; *Wiltshire dialect*

Thoughts on Public Transport; *trip to London*

Archie and the Haiku; *for Archie and his Mum*

Florence's Pie; *Terry Wogan comes to The Black Swan*

Supermarkets

The Devizing of a Plan; *regarding the Devizes Neighbourhood Plan referendum*

Choosing Choice; *and again*

Drawing a Line; for Hayley Nutland; *Hayley plays a blinder*

Moonraker Bears; *for the Moonraker Bears shop in Sidmouth Street*

A Devizes Quimmerick; *someone said something dodgy about Trowbridge girls*

Lost and Found; the Spurious Incident of the Dog in the Night Time; *for Helen*

Assize Matters

Shopping with Claire Perry; *where Claire Perry MP is touched at Morrisons*

Back Seat Joker; *that bus*

Tumbleweed; *concerns about charging for the usage of the Market Place*

All White

teen spirit; a tanka; *that bus again*

Trippin' on the 101; *bus plus*

Bollards in the Market Place

trowbridge; a tanka

The Mysterious Tankards of Dunkirk Hill

Cheaper Chips; for Jeffersons; *for Jeffersons in Monday Market Street*

Intolerance

Mistaken Identity

Computing Rhythm

Scary Beatle rock
Style, venom and melody
Blue soul crashing sound

Computing rhythm
Turning tables, turning air
Too cool for old school

Riff of rebellion
Tidy, tight, provocative
Rattling of The Bin

Whasson, You?

Words from Wiltshire
Hard to define all
You say Mildenhall
And I say Minal
"Ere, whasson?"
We say in Wiltshire
"Ere, areet then?"
"Mine's a 6Xy beer"
"Catch you laters…"
(Sorry, when?)

Thoughts on Public Transport

Pewsey Hills

mist of Vale rising

unclothing hills of ivory

revealing glory

The Train Cuckoo

In the Reserved seats,

elsewhere by fate diverted,

invisible men;

weather, lover's bed or grave?

What cares the cuckoo for why?

Wroughton

Over

Wrought

On

The

Bus

Archie and the Haiku

Today I met a small boy called Archie at the Devizes Street Festival. He came in on a conversation about haiku, saying that he had written some at school. He began concentrating on composing a haiku. He came up with the first line and then counted syllables on his fingers thoughtfully, for some time. After a while, and much furrowing of his brow, the music got louder, an ice cream appeared in front of him and we came up with this:

a wet rainy day -
small boy writing poetry
looking at ice cream

Well done, Archie, a good lad who knows that haiku are fun...

Florence's Pie

No traffic jam when Terry came
No culinary surprise
He used his loaf and found some cheese
When munching round The Vize
He and his little Mason friend
Had breakfast at The Bear
Sausage, bacon, beans an ting
No revelation there
Terry chewed the fat a bit
And did a bit of walking
A bit of pork, a bit of cake
And pudding (now you're talking)
The flight of locks left Terry cold
He didn't eat the quackers
Then things got quite interesting
When John got out his clackers
And hold on there is Florence
Making Olde Vizes Pie
Terry's buds are tickled now
A stuffed fox winks an eye

So cheers for that then, Terry, mate
You put our town on telly
But next time have some lardy
And get rat arsed in the Pelly

Supermarkets

One day I went to Morrisons
Forgot to take a map
I only wanted beans and buns
And bog roll for a crap
Got lost by the ladies things
Forgot my North and South
I didn't come for flapping wings
Or stuff to wash the mouth
It's just as bad in Sainsburys
Perhaps it is my age
The fruitless quest for herbal teas
Just puts me in a rage
I'm far too flipping old for these
Daily shopping trials
I'm sweating like a Stilton cheese
Lost in the British aisles
Maybe home delivery?
Should I? Do I dare?
Become a couch potato
Fat arsed, shopping from my chair
I'd miss the talking checkout though
And cheery orange bags
My unexpected items
And my special pricey fags
I'm hard, I can handle it
I'm such a little trooper
And while I'm there I'll have a shit
Markets. Simply Super.

The Devizing of a Plan

All careful plans of men may fail and fall
And falter, crumble; leaving broken stone
No reason to devise no plan at all
For no man lives by wild chance alone
There has been an edict from on high
"Thou shalt build houses here within ten years
Three hundred homes and thirty three." Then why
Not have a say and ease those planning fears
This Plan has seemed quite hard to understand
To many folk irrelevant, a bore
Yet now the vital hour is at hand
The issue far too pressing to ignore
"What consultation has there been?" the voice
Comes from the floor, comes loud and with an edge
"No one told us that we had a choice
And where are all the leaflets, in the hedge?"
It goes like this; the Trust have made a plan
Consulted up the Brittox, in the post
Collated all the info, then began
To work out where we wanted homes the most
They spoke with parish councils, factored in
The traffic, schools, the shops and open space
They put in measures to avoid the sin
Of building ugly stuff that spoils the place
Without the Plan the builders have free rein
To ride roughshod across our lovely land
At which point, just don't bother to complain
The horse has bolted, galloping, unmanned
If jobs for boys there are let them be ours
Let local builders lay their firm foundations
On brownfield sites, not green fields full of flowers
With guidelines from the Plan's considerations

No plan is perfect; yet no plan at all

Will simply give us no control, not clever

Consider this; vote Yes at the Town Hall

Or mourn the loss of favoured fields, forever

Choosing Choice

My alarm clock shouts at me with noisy voice
"Wake up! It's Thursday and you have a choice!"
Of what to have for breakfast, eggs or bran
And of voting or not voting on the Plan
I'm not that sure quite what it's all about
Perhaps I'll go online and check it out
The library know their stuff, they're pretty fair
Could ask at the Town Hall, there's people there
That funny poet woman says "Vote Yes"
Or otherwise the town will be a mess
Without a Plan we just won't have a clue
Of what outside developers will do
But other folk are saying "No! Vote No!"
I'm so confused about which way to go
If I don't vote I haven't had a say
It's only a few moments from my day
I'm going to go to town now and the Market
Could take the car but it's a job to park it
Might take my bike or simply take a walk
And wander round and meet some friends and talk
I wonder what they think, I'll ask their views
They might, like me, be wondering what to choose
Meat from the butchers, or some humble spam
Or whether to have a quick one in The Lamb
I've chosen breakfast eggs, I'm on a roll
I'm going to town, I'm going to simply stroll
I'm going to look at options and take note
I'm choosing choice and I am going to vote

If stuff goes wrong I've got till ten o'clock
The day is long, I'm on it (where's that sock?)

Drawing a Line; for Hayley Nutland

The word on the street is that Hayley done good
A considerable feat for the girl from the wood
She caught him, she taught him, that crime doesn't pay
She sought him, she fought him, he got put away
There are good folk and bad folk, it's not always clear
Some folk have a toke, and drink buckets of beer
But at mugging and stabbing, this girl draws a line
She witnessed the grabbing, gave chase, and done fine
So think twice when you say that someone is a zero
Today, doff your hat, because Hayley's a hero

Moonraker Bears

'Tis the night before Sunday, the bears are awake

Excited and hungry for lunchtime and cake

They are Moonraker Bears, and quite partial to cheese

Hanging out at the Crammer and hiding in trees

The word in the cupboard, in bunk beds and chairs

Is that Giles is coming to talk about bears

There'll be new bears and old bears, all having a chat

Discussing the look of this coat and that hat

And the children will be there, the children are nice

Someone might buy a bear for a reasonable price

A new friend for Paddington, Winnie or Ted

Who might come home to stay on the chair or the bed

There's a doctor for sick bears, a hospital too

And a website for bears that is totally new

About time, said the teddies, a place just for us

Where we bears can hang out without worry or fuss

We can't wait till it opens, to go there and play

At the Moonraker Bears shop, down Sidmouth Street way

A Devizes Quimmerick

I know men, young and old, from Devizes

Who are wolves in surprising disguises

Sometimes girls are as bad

But it's often the lad

Who, for whoring, has shelves full of prizes

Pretty Trowbridge girls, all in a row

There will always be one that's a ho

And some may like a lay

But not all of them, hey

Just maybe the ones that you know

So, fine upstanding men from Devizes

Rendered 'helpless' by fit pairs of thighses

Be more cautious when drunk

More in charge of your sp*nk

Less "Not me, it was her, with her eyeses"

Lost and Found; the Spurious Incident of the Dog in the Night Time

Who's in the dog house, someone has been flakey

The someone who lost the unfortunate Jakey

Thank heavens for Girls and the Book of the Face

And the people of town who live down Mayenne Place

For needles in haystacks are easy to spot

Compared to the dog who was there, and was not

The tale of his loss was inherently spurious

The dog in the night time; an incident curious

They shouted, they whistled, they got out their torches

Searched the canal and the shadows in porches

Where was the Jakey dog? No one could tell

Till somebody heard a desperate yell

"He's here" someone said, "he's been here all night"

Oh dear, someone will be in the dog house tonight

Result; one happy girl and a tail wagging hound

And 'The dog which was lost' now 'The dog which was found'

Assize Matters; a Fairy Tale

Once upon a time there was a grand historical building, in the centre of a small but beautiful Wiltshire town, called the Assize Court. For many years the processes of law were carried out within the stern Bath stone walls of the Court, and many folk were sentenced in the dock. Some walked under the Ionic pillars to freedom, some to death and some to endless captivity. All human drama was there. Tears fell to stony ground, reputations were ruined and children were left fatherless. Justice was seen to be done. But then one day, as is the way of things, it became obsolete; the last sentence was delivered, and the doors were closed. It stood, slowly decaying, for year upon year; a strange symbol of dereliction in the beating heart of the town. And now, and then, good folk devoted much energy to finding new hope and purpose for the building. Nothing came to pass. The people were met by brick walls and stonewalling. People gave up the fight. It crumbled. Years, and yet more years, passed. Good folk tried again. No joy. More brick walls and stone walling. It crumbled. Again, passionate people rallied, and tried to make sense of it. Again, brick walls and stonewalling. It crumbled. Until, one day, it had crumbled beyond all hope. At which point the land was used to build houses and offices. And yea, verily, as some had prophesied, someone made a large pot of gold. And lived happily ever after.

Shopping with Claire Perry

If you don't care for Claire

Don't touch her there

She's really a bit of a toff

Some mouths are wide

To fit poor folk inside

And some Tory stuff

Might rub off

Oh, buyer beware

When you're shopping with Claire

Maybe wear a nice hat you can doff

And take her advice

On the bog roll and rice

You buy one, you get one

BOGOF

Back Seat Joker

Effing this, and jeffing that

Another bus, another twat

Impressing peers with his wit

Sort of. Slightly. Just a bit.

Drop the 'c' bomb, hey why not

Girls will think you're really hot

Louder, lad, we want to hear

About the weed and drugs and beer

You smoke and deal and snort and sup

How you get high and then throw up

That college bores you to a yawn

That bigger breasts make better porn

Ooh, a word that rhymes with tank

Have we got Tourette's to thank

For the verbal diarrhoea

You pour in to our captive ear

Or are you, sunshine, simply rude

Insecure, pathetic, lewd

Wow, a word that rhymes with sock

Shouted loud to cause a shock

Tits and fanny, bell end, bum

Words you wouldn't say to Mum

What makes you think we want to know

That so and so is just a ho

That your best mate's a massive tool

It's just like being back at school

There's no escape, we're on the bus

We've got to listen to you cuss

All the way to flippin' town

Please lad, turn the volume down

Before I stand and loud recite

This rhyme I felt compelled to write

Inspired by the irritation

Caused by your inane oration

The bus is crawling up Dunkirk

My poem will keep, you're just a jerk

Ah, the joys of middle age

Intolerance, indignant rage

Imagine if I'd read the verse

I'd have been like you but worse

So not the time or place for it

Back seat joker, talking shit

tumbleweed; a haiku

winter; market place
the carnival is over
there be tumbleweed

All White

Today I met a Cockney friend
In a right old nark
He'd just got a ticket, said
"What's with the parking lark?"
He wasn't up for Station Road
Said "What's that all about
I want a place to park, mate
Not a trainspotter's day out"
Then he mentioned something
About some plates of meat
So I took the bloke to Walter Rose
The one up Sidmouth Street
He looked a bit surprised when he
Was faced with trays of pork
"Geezer, knock it on the head
Don't you know Cockney talk?
I left him looking for a girl
Who wasn't known to me
He was meeting her at Brogans
Said, her name was Rosie Lee
I got some Christmas shopping
And thought about my chum
We hadn't hit it off today
I really felt quite glum
Tonight while in the Market Place
I bumped in to my mate
He'd been drinking beer and whisky
And was in a tipsy state
I'll tell you what" he says, "mate
You're a little Christmas light
And, pointing at some buildings, said
"All white, mate, you're all white"

teen spirit; a tanka

smells like teen spirit

the impulse and ammonia

lynx and mary jane

heated hormone heavy air

fogs the windows of the bus

Trippin' on the 101

So, when staffing levels are low on local buses they let 'that guy' out of the cupboard. Many years ago, when he drove another bus, he stopped down a lonely road deep in the wilds and suggested that the only passengers, a docile and pretty vulnerable looking girl and I, disembark and have a 'fag'. He responded to refusal and rollicking with bemusement, and stated that he felt misunderstood. He has appeared on various buses sporadically since. Today he drove the 101. The 101 is a loveable, much valued, slightly odd and erratic service that ferries workers, students and commuters between towns. We need it real bad. Mostly it turns up. The drivers are invariably pleasant and helpful in a monosyllabic kind of way. Journeys happen. There is the odd thwarted connection and infrequent annoyance. There are occasional amusements. It chugs along, and usually does what it says on the rusty tin. Sometimes bits fall off. It has been known to be over familiar with stationary objects. You know where you are with the 101. Clanking between towns, or standing at a bus stop watching the tumbleweed roll.

But every now and again they get one out of the cupboard. And today it was 'that guy'.

The bus driving is merely a sideline. He's all about the comedy, the over familiarity, the inappropriate quip, the seamless narrative and the ironic joy of the journey. He talks, loudly, all the way, delivering a bizarre and overfamiliar monologue to the whole bus. It's a guided tour and we, my friends, are captive to the ride. As each person embarks he makes a pithy remark about their presumed relationship status and choice of domicile. "Welcome to the City of Dreams", he chimes, as we enter Bogley. At one point he outlines, in his stream of noisy consciousness, the different reasons we might be travelling on the bus, which include "Perhaps you can't afford the parking fees." Shoppers, commuters, students and wage slaves, some familiar with 'that guy' and some not, exchange knowing smirks, raised eyebrows and puzzlement. It's hard to assess the situation. He must be OK to drive, surely, or they wouldn't let him...would they? Could he be having an 'episode'? Are we in mortal danger? Is he for real? Are we? Is he just a 'character'? Should nutters drive buses? And is the use of the word 'nutter' indicative of prejudice? It's all very confusing, and the more complicated passengers experience an uncomfortable cognitive dissonance. He is talking to his mirror now, to all of us, about everything and nothing in particular. No-one catches his eye, but he is impervious to rejection. He just carries on carrying on. Just before my leap for freedom at the bus stop he thanks us all effusively for travelling with him, and hopes that he will see us all again on Monday. We don't know what to say. An empty can that once held an energy drink rolls down the aisle from the back of the bus.

Quirk is good. Random entertainment is sometimes an unexpected delight. Comedy counts. Everyone likes a grey day to be brightened with fun. We all need friends. We all want to be loved. We would, mostly, hesitate to judge, lest we be judged. We all want individuality and creativity to be encouraged. But not on the way home from work on the bus. We want to worry about our relationships and bank balances. We want to look out of the window mournfully and play with our phones. We want to fantasise about our weekend and its anticipated delights. We don't want to think that someone has spiked us with acid by the water cooler. Or that we have been transported to a world inhabited by scary pixies. Or that we may never get home. Really.

So. You're funny alright, mate, in a peculiar sort of way. You may well mean well. You could, quite possibly be harmless. Your irregular and unusual appearance is certainly mentally stimulating. But please, for the love of all things understandable, put a flippin' sock in it and just drive the bus.

Public transport matters. The number 101. You couldn't make it up. So I didn't.

Bollards in the Market Place

Stuff's happening in the Market Place
To really make folk cuss
Why isn't there a parking space
And where's the f*cking bus?
The traffic lights are stuck on red
It shouldn't be like this
Park down Station Road instead?
Don't take the flippin' piss
The long drive in from Long Street
Is a journey one may rue
Traffic jam, and save the feet
Or walk, and dodge the poo?
There are barriers by the chip shop
And the road looks really odd
Where can the hungry driver stop
To score a battered cod?
And, catch a bus outside the Bear?
That's seriously confusing
A pop up pick up bus stop, where?
Change is not amusing
Damn those blokes in hi vis coats
For getting in the way
Some fat cat who got our votes
Has dug up Market Day
Why can't it happen overnight
Can someone wave a wand
And some strange flowing spell recite
Whilst mooning by the pond
Disrupted traffic, vain appeals
Bring back the bloody station!
Angry faces mouth at wheels
Expressions of frustration

Call them bloody roadworks

When the bloody road ain't working?

More bollards than a Corn Bin night

Just a bit less twerking

trowbridge; a tanka

grey skies drop gruel
shoppers shelter in the shires
drinking weather, spoons
whatever, raining, trowbridge
pea soup puddled county town

The Mysterious Tankards of Dunkirk Hill

Four tankards found at the foot of the hill

Bet someone got w*nkered, and now they feel ill

Bet it went down so easy that no one resisted

And now they've forgotten the tankards existed

But down at the pub there are rumours of scandals

Of boisterousness, and the theft of four candles

And a gap on the shelf where the tankards once sat

And out on the roof someone's comedy hat

Maybe barred from the pub and a walk out of town?

With enough beer in tow to conceivably drown

As they woke up the town with their loud shouty glee

And blessed all the hedges with vomit and pee

"Here's bashin' yer metal" and "Cheers, me old china"

Drinking alfresco, well, what could be finer

Well, ale, I suppose, for it goes down a treat

Not that one cares when one's drunk on the street

The next day the tankards just sat by the road

All hopeful and waiting, but nobody showed

Until round the corner a giant appeared

Wearing a rugby shirt, smile and beard

"I'll tell you what, lads, all back to mine"

Four trusting tankards all followed in line

Expressing their heartfelt and infinite thanks

With tinkles, and clatters, and resonant clanks

There followed a search, and some transient glory

And some vain attempt to uncover their story

So brightly they shone in their moment of fame

Then they just disappeared, in the way that they came

'Tis said, down in Rowde, that the veil is thin

That mischievous fairies throw stuff in the bin

That strange things do happen, when folk have been drinking

All myth mixed with moonshine and magical thinking

Whatever, wherever, they're not coming back

So; whose were the tankards, and what was the crack?

Cheaper Chips; for Jeffersons

I went to Jeffersons one day
The atmosphere was nice and easy
A cup of tea they gave away
With tasty chips, all hot and cheesy
It's as-you-like-it-as-it-comes
A warm old fashioned friendly caff
Simple grub for hungry tums
That's not too posh and not too naff
An unpretentious jolly place
Just comfort food served fast and hot
No silly gimmicks in your face
Spinach sprinkles? I think not
I'm partial to a cheaper chip
So Jeffersons will do for me
I only left a tiny tip
So they can have my rhyme for free

Intolerance

She greets us with loud and American brightness
Gives us the menu with florid politeness
Has cheerfulness written all over her face
But just hasn't quite got the tone of the place
We only went in there to grab a quick brunch
But seemingly we have a threesome for lunch
As she spoons out her unsubtle dollops of chatter
Outlining the options for every platter
So much information, and so much to say
About this, about that, about soup of the day
Every tale of the menu she's tempted to tell
Bless her, she's on it, and on us as well

He raises an eyebrow, and I raise one back
An unspoken agreement to cut her some slack
Till she asks us what we are intolerant to
At which point he coughs, and I go to the loo
She's nice, oh she's nice enough, don't get me wrong
We're just dreading the moment she bursts in to song
If we want a McDonalds, we'll bear her in mind
But we came here for something profound, and refined
Alfafa, and silence, and spiced meditation
Weird stuff on salad, profound conversation
To gaze from the window, like, mournful and arty
Invisible guests at a well tasteful party

Instead there is her, with her zest and her zing
Motivating our order with...
"Let's do this thing!"

Mistaken Identity

I've been likened to many people in my life; Nerys Hughes, Jack Wild, Chrissie Hynde, and others. I have been mistaken for a bloke a few times, and a one-eyed woman ten years older than me once. In recent years people have mixed up me and the lovely Mary Van Riemsdyk on frequent occasions. But today this happened...

I'm by the fountain taking photographs. The light is shining through the streams of the fountain most pleasingly. I manage to get a shot of the statue of Ceres through the trees and the spurting spouts. I am wearing me poet rags and a look of deranged obsession, nicely accessorised with a scowl.

I hear a voice, and it says...

"Are you Claire Perry?"

Claire Perry is the Conservative Member of Parliament for Devizes.

...?

I turn, and see a well-heeled and strangely charismatic elderly gentleman. He is sporting a rather unusual and jaunty pair of spectacles with blue glass lenses that hide what I presume to be a twinkle in his eye.

"Did you just call me Claire Perry?" says I as I walk up to him. There's a challenge if ever there was one.

"Yes," he says "you look like her."

...?

I inform him that I am highly amused, that he has made my day, and that I will be putting his comment on Facebook. I shake his hand (I'm a hearty hand shaker). I ask him his first name, and tell him mine, at which point he says...

"Clearly you are not Claire Perry."

"No" says I.

"You should be so lucky!" he says, as he walks away.

I laugh all the way home.

Clearly I need to rethink my look.

Lol. Big fat massive side splitting lol. Claire Perry indeed.

Still laughing.

Death and Epitaphs

Rosemary's Funeral

Before the Gate; *for her*

So Nearly There; *for K*

Gone

Infinite Stars; *for Margaret Osborne*

David Osborne's Funeral; Scrubbing Up Well

Invisible Man

truly odd; a bowie thing

Too Late For Words

Brides Mound; for Kathy Hope

Blossom Rising; *on the deaths of Major John Cairns Bartholomew and a much loved tree*

Farewell, Father Jack

Scatter Me

Waiting for Her

Howard Marks; a Clerihew

Wasted Angels

Rosemary's Funeral

My mother's coffin on the bier, up the cobbled steps to St. Mary's church. My babe folded warm to my breast. Green turf on the hill and the early cry of lambs upon the Plain. Warm breath, warm wind, the knell of an ancient bell, solemn steps up to the sacred temple, dedicated to His mother, The Mother, all mothers, my mother.

For Spring is a dying in itself. My child stirs. She waited for him before her passing. I pressed him to her breast as she lay dying, her window open, bright gifted daffodils a-stirring on the sill. I took a photograph and have it still. My mother, blessed in her helplessness, still fierce in her humility, with a twinkle in her eye, a warm smile and her only grandchild in her arms.

Funeral over and back in the light my son and I await new life.

Before the Gate

"What say you, Woman?"
As she stands before the gate
"That I loved" she said

So Nearly There

Painted man, upon your skin
Danced pictures of your coloured past
Hard on the outside, sweet within
Through storm and sunshine you held fast
To love of friends and hope of light
Knowing of a better way
Trusting the morn to follow night
And hands to wipe your tears away

You were like us, both good and bad
Made of joy and painful things
Like all of us, we knew you had
Both devil's horns and angel's wings
So many words are left unsaid
Your life a short unfinished prayer
For happiness and your own bed
So nearly there, so nearly there

gone

curtain flutter
candle sputter
gone

Infinite Stars; for Margaret and David

She sees her love in the infinite stars

In a billion light years, a breath away

In Vincent's swirls and the eddies of night

Oh stay, my dear love, stay

She hears in the darkness a distant bell

Vibrating through the cosmic sea

Lulling her lover to fathoms of sleep

Oh stay, my love, with me

She feels his imprint on the bed

The hollowed space, the empty glove

In the silence of night she prays for grace

Oh stay, with me, my love

She knows that she knew him utterly

As she folds the clothes that clothed a star

Alone and together in infinite light

So near, my love, so far

David's Osborne's Funeral; Scrubbing Up Well

We have said farewell to David

How we wish he had been there

To see how much we loved the sod

And how we did our hair

He would have loved the eulogy

In which he got a mention

For David always loved to be

The centre of attention

He would have liked the humour

Had a hanky for the tears

Been astounded at the love he had

To show for all his years

He would have wept to see us weeping

Would have made a funny joke

Not one much for nonsense

A 'geezer' sort of bloke

A man who worked with chemistry

Who painted and played chess

Who liked music and black humour

And admired a pretty dress

Two different lives, three families

So many made the trip

From different worlds, from far away

His blood, his fellowship

He would have loved the readings

Would have looked well to this day

And nodded at Corinthians

In a wise and knowing way

He would have said "Look after Margaret"

And run after Michelle

Then winked at Dick, and hugged his son

And others he knew well

I thought I saw him in the corner

Saw him sitting in a chair

Serenity personified

For just a moment there

He really loved 'Jerusalem'

We sang that bugger loud

My God, we scrubbed up bloody well

And did the bugger proud

Invisible Man

He stood upon the chair

A knotted rope

Around his neck

All passion spent

Just waiting

For the fall

I never understood, he thought

What others meant

Or why nobody

Quite

Got me

At all

A better place, he thought

Away from

Violent pain

Loss

Misery

And sin

And no one

Saw him

Going out

Like no one

Saw him

Coming in

truly odd; a bowie thing

something strange to earth was sent
dropped some art then simply went
now lonely spiders left on mars
watch red shoes dance on dusty stars
and walls of televisions sing
sweet things about the rebel king
the lad insane, the skinny duke
androgynous inspired fluke
flight of peacock, coloured flash
funkin' funky ash to ash
china diamond, cold as god
genuinely, truly odd

Too Late For Words

Oh, when they were alive we never said
The things we say about them now they're dead
Too far away now, too far gone to hear
Gone, never to return or reappear
Too late to say how much they meant to us
Just hollow words, and funerals, and fuss
And sorry tears, and memories, and pain
And wishing we could see their face again
That gaze exchanged by eyes when last we met
That lingered a split second, we forget
That precious image, vague, so hard to find
In corner cupboards of unconscious mind

Why didn't we just tell them they were great
Too late today, too late now, all too late
We had that thought that day, we didn't call
What if we never called that much at all
Or when we did, droned on and on and on
No chance to listen now they're dead and gone
And our last words, a blessing or a curse?
A dirty joke or elevating verse?

And what if it was bad, so very bad
Unreasonably difficult or sad
Too late to shake hands now, forget, forgive
For they have gone and we have stayed to live
To reconcile our difference alone
With icy wind and cold unyielding stone
With questioning, with anger, fear and prayer
And all the time just wishing they were there
They change us most, our dearest kith and kin
Lay waste the landscapes that we dwell within
Leave shattered palaces in ruined wake
Leave with that part of us they chose to take

Make waves rise up on ponds in silent glades
Blast particles of light through sunken shades
Part oceans with their leaving, break the sky
Leave fish upon the shore line high and dry

And even those we never thought we knew
The ones we thought were simply passing through
However long the number of their days
Do change us, in small subtle little ways
Make dust prints on the table in the hall
Leave crumbs on plates, and scuff marks on the wall
Blow gentle breezes soft through window crack
That whisper 'I am never coming back'

The more we loved the more we miss, the more
We yearn for some strange loophole in the law
Unwilling to concede the battle lost
To pay for love, and ever count the cost
We search in dream, in lonely mountain walk
For one last touch, for one last quiet talk
And briefly, in the corner of our eye
We see them come, and go, and wave goodbye

At every funeral we stand and swear
That next time we will say how much we care
Say that we love them, call them on the phone
To let them know that they are not alone
And every time we fail and forget
That well intentioned heartfelt course we set
I loved you, did you know that, tell me true?
Unanswered echoes coming back at you
Dark holes within the soul and endless night
Bright angels lost in distant blinding light
The empty vase, the upturned empty chair
Deep lesions of the heart and songs in air

Bride's Mound; for Kathy Hope

Up on Bride's Mound, where the sky meets the ground

Circle wheels within wheels, on a blue winter day

Child of the trees, of the stars and the breeze

How much we love her and want her to stay

Waft of incense on air, words of ritual prayer

Gentleness, blessing, children at play

They who confessed her, who laid out and dressed her

Scattering acorns, wormwood, and bay

No dark corner spared in the memories shared

Of the pain that she had before finding her way

Rivers of sound, through the harp, through the ground

Diluting the darkness, dissolving dismay

Herein is forgiving; the dead and the living

Made fresh by the scent of a rosemary spray

And redemption and peace, in her final release

Leave us free to remember and love as we may

We are all of us here, she has nothing to fear

Her spirit has gone from the bier where she lay

As together we stand, on this green hallowed land

Holding dear Kathy Hope as we love her away

Blossom Rising; on the death of Major John Cairns Bartholomew, and a much loved tree

Beneath a grey and monumental sky
In wild confetti clouds that dance in air
The blossom falls; all trees and men will die
However good, or beautiful, or rare

For years, beneath the branches of that tree
Have lovers kissed, have lonely mourners waited
All men and trees shall die; he, thee, and me
By that same force destroyed and yet created

The clattering of horses' hooves, the sound
Of yeoman passing, ghosts that haunt the ears
All trees and men returneth to the ground
'Till from the light new word of life appears

In red Victorian brick and petal glow
Are strength and beauty blended 'fore our eyes
Good men and trees in season come and go
Such knowledge is the glory of the wise

Drink with your eyes each bright delight you see
And savour every moment of creation
For man will pass and wind will fell the tree
And wine will drop on coffins in libation

While blood still flows like sap, best drain your glass
Enjoy the fleeting sunbeam in your ale
For trees and men shall die; for all things pass
All moonlight fade and colours turn to pale

Let hops be gathered; make of sunshine, hay
Add rosebuds and ferment a heady brew
For trees and men shall certain pass away
As dark of midnight shadows summer's blue

For soon enough last orders will be rung
Sad flags will flutter half way up the mast
Dark laments for men and trees be sung
And rest be found for dear old souls at last

Learn wisdom, child, from ale and wood and bone

Brew love in barrels down in cellars deep

And find it there when you return, alone

To watch the man in blossom rise from sleep

Farewell Father Jack; a clerihew

So, farewell then, Father Jack

Let this be writ upon a plaque

"All things pass;

Drink, feck, arse..."

Scatter Me

Scatter me there where the winds are sweet
To the blue of the sky and the sun's bright heat
On Oliver's Camp where the dragon lines meet
Scatter me there on the hill

Scatter me there where the waters flow
Where the weeping mourners come and go
Down by The Wharf where the ducklings grow
Scatter me there on the bridge

Scatter me there where the earth sees all
When the pond is lit by a moonbeam's fall
Where the children play and the drunkards brawl
Scatter me there on the green

Scatter me there where the griffons play
Where the waters pour the hours away
In the pool of the fountain on Market Day
Scatter me there in the stream

Scatter me there with the silent dead
Where ages of souls have been buried and wed
And the angels cavort among coffins of lead
Scatter me there by the church

Scatter me there where the townsfolk cried
And strew flowers on the steps when Diana died
In the place where 'tis said that Ruth Pierce lied
Scatter me there on the cross

Scatter me here and leave me be
On every street, under every tree
Until I am dust and memory
Scatter me here where I'm free

Waiting for Her

They waited for her

The undertakers

The thin scatter of mourners

The silent deceased

Waited

As the wind battered the roof of the crematorium

Waited

As mourners waiting with another coffin wept outside

Waited

For her

To come and read his eulogy

For her

To do him justice with her friendly words

Waited

On the direst and most miserable March day there ever was

Waited

And she never came

Howard Marks; a Clerihew

So, farewell, Howard, Mr Nice
Massive reefers were your vice
Life's but a spliff to puff and pass
All grass is weed, all flesh is grass

Wasted Angels

Howard Marks and God Almighty
Shared a spliff, and had a whitey
Then had the munchies, and a bong
Annoying Peter with the pong
By which time it was far too late
To frisk young Howard at the gate
God, seeing Peter's consternation
Outlined the process of creation
How on day three he made the weed
With every other tree and seed
To raise in some, apotheosis
And test some others, with psychosis

Now, Howard's stash was pretty small
And didn't last too long at all
So, as he didn't see the point
Of heaven's joys without a joint
He got his bong, and skins, and tin
Chucked all the roaches in the bin
And, following a wicked smell
Went wafting off to score, in hell

St. Peter looked above and groaned
As all the angels flew past, stoned

Faffing About On Facebook; in which I am enraged and amused, and moved to pen vulgar verse

The Troll

Tree Humour

Fie Sir, thou art a Troll; *trolls...so rude*

Britain First

The Mystic Aardvark

Faithless Flake

Not Much On The Telly; *the Croydon Gazette reports an unusual protest about nothing in particular*

Wotsits; *a response to a picture of a girl in a bath of Worsits*

Cyber Wank; *it's not big and it's not clever*

Gnawing Resentment

Monster Twat; *to the tune of 'Monster Mash'*

Crap Hackers; for Andy Paine

Family Shopping; *something untoward happens in a shop in broad daylight*

Christ and the Badly Written Atheist Rhyme

Just Write Well; *The Writers Group*

haiku haiku; *Writers Group haiku smack down*

narcissus and the carp; a tanka; *massive troll*

A Bad Poem About Faeces

Tubuktim

The Issues In Devizes Poetry Slam; *thanks for the laughs*

Scat Magician

The Troll

Fol de rol, quoth the troll with the bell on his cap

Tell me your soul, come and fall in my lap

Does the mole in the hole have a map of the trap?

Is a troll on a roll just like crap on a bap?

Tree Humour

One joke about ash might be comedy cash
Bash on about oak and leave comedy broke
Tree humour: a) corny but b) each to his own
For the mightiest joke from a seedling is grown

Fie, Sir, thou art a Troll

Your voyeuristic anal post
Has got me choking on my toast
I should have better things to do
Than commenting on sex and poo
Whilst everybody likes a joke
'Tis somewhat niche, the anal poke
Night up the alley, hard to see
For those without a front door key
What people do behind closed doors
With wives or husbands, friends or whores
Is up to them when with consent
I question, sir, your post's intent
We English hide within our castles
No comment when it comes to assholes
Trolling really gets my goat
Fie, sir, flounder in my moat
I hope your banal gasket's blown
Write what you know, and get your own

Britain First

Britain First, on cabbage gnawing
Tasteless racists, bigots, boring
Watch them chew on racist beef
With bits of cabbage on their teeth

The Mystic Aardvark

Alan the Mystic

Aardvark

Rejected wrath and

Drama

Violence and ire

Alan said

Result in endless

Karma

Faithless Flake

Many flakes

It takes to make

A snowman

Little sisters

Little brothers

Make no mistake

Flakes melt and cake

And some are flakier

Than others

The silent fake

For it's own sake

May replicate

One then another

And float to ground

Without a sound

To lie unfound

A faithless

Lover

Not Much On The Telly

I woke up this morning

And had a bright idea

I'll glue my arse to Debenhams

When I've had some beer

Then I'll give the public

A big piece of my mind

Stick Dennis on my Menace

On the front of my behind

There's nothing on the telly

And I like to have a shout

I'm the Talent Britain's Got

Check my beaver out

Nothing much to see here

That's big news to me

I'm the bargain of the day

Take me home for free

I met that Westwood woman once

I win hands down for style

Talk about the ex factor

I took the bloke on Kyle

Last week I did Poundland

I'm simply effing class

I'm the prat who with a Pritt Stick

Glued a window to her arse

What's The Crack With The Wotsits?

What's under

The Wotsits

I wonder?

When did cheese

Ever please

Going under?

What a laugh

Take a barf

Have a chunder

Going down

You may drown

What a blunder

You can bet

She'll expect

You to fund her

Insalubrious

Dubious

Plunder

Cyber Wank

You took a break from masturbation
To indulge in provocation
Badly judged, son, what bad luck
For most of us don't give a f*ck
Now that you've expressed your issues
Best clean up with man sized tissues
We're writers, kid, we're hard as nails
Pointless posts and epic fails
Provide our mills with grist to write
For we make gold dust out of shite
So thanks for your ejaculate
If you were hoping for some hate
You'll get some now, so good for you
You'll get some love and humour too
And feedback and some cyber hugging...

Have you logged off now?
Bet you're tugging...

Gnawing Resentment

He gnawed on his resentment
In public and alone
Like a dog he kept on worrying
The marrow from the bone
Till he gave himself an ulcer
Till his teeth got small and stumpy
Till other dogs said, Hang on, Fang
You're starting to look grumpy
He wouldn't leave the thing alone
Just wouldn't let it lie
Time to put the bone down, Fido
Go on, try

Monster Twat

I was having itchy fingers the other day

At the same time as I saw something I took the wrong way

My bile rose and I started to play

I spewed out a rhyme and I had my say

I was a twat

I was a total twat

I put it on the internet

Just like that

I was a twat

Better eat my hat

I was a twat....

I pressed the angry button and I just let fly

There was red mist all around me and a plank in my eye

I usually know better and I usually try

To keep an eye on karma and my powder dry

But this time...

I've been a twat

I've been a total twat

I stick my hands up to it

Just like that

I've been a twat

One has been a prat

I've been a twat...

So I hope I've learned my lesson with my recent fail

Don't be quite so quick to comment, brew a lighter ale

And if I really must then just don't leave a trail

Stay as hard as a lettuce and as soft as a nail

Don't be a twat

I mustn't be a twat

It won't go well at all

If I act like that

Won't be a twat

Now I feel better for that

But still a twat....

Crap Hackers

Who's been hacking Andy?
Someone who's quite sick
A sad pathetic wanker
Who just couldn't find his dick
There are some tossers out there
They don't half crack off some shite
Bored and boring little men
Crap shadows in the night
Nothing else to do I guess
A proper little charmer
Our Andy just knocks spots off you
So good luck with your karma

Family Shopping

What you doing, Mummy?

(cue a stifled cough)

I'm just sniffing Daddy

And I think he's going off

But you're always doing that, Mum

Making Daddy's face go red

Can't you get some sweeties, or

Some chewing gum instead

Are we nearly there yet?

We're really bored, we'd rather

Piss about in Poundland

Than be playing 'how's yer father'

Shut up kids, we're nearly done

Hey, stand back, Daddy's popping

Don't ever say we don't have fun

Doing the family, shopping

Christ and the Badly Written Atheist Rhyme

Talk to the hand, said Christ

You're absurd

At least I turned up

With an interesting Word

Remember, I came

Not with peace but the sword

So cut out the crap

Because frankly I'm bored

You say atheists

Are nicer than me

Some of them probably are

I agree

But really I wonder

Quite whether you

Have anything much

Of interest to do

Get back to me when

You have something to say

In the meantime I'm busy

And wish you good day

Just Write Well

So much flouncing

And denouncing

In this heaven

That is hell

Best to polish yourself

So the shit slips off

And

Just Write Well

haiku; a haiku

winter; writers' rain
dripping haiku in to pools
crystallising light

narcissus and the carp; a tanka

narcissus, the pond

across the surface ripples

disillusionment

dead in the water, floating

not so koi now, bloated carp

A Bad Poem About Faeces

As a species

We do faeces

Really well

As for writers

Some are shiter

And can't spell

Writing, shiting

All the same

I hear you shout

For with either

Stuff goes in

And stuff

Comes out

Tubuktim

My view on Timbuktu is this

I don't know where the f*ck it is

Some odd foreign far off land

With naff all shops and lots of sand

Three scabby camels and a tree

Hey, I get lost in Swindon, me

So sod the bare and thirsty hills

F*ck me, you'd have to be Bear Grylls

I've seen him pissing on his hat

Not sure I'm really up for that

And bog roll? Not in Timbuktu

Endless plains without a loo

And nowhere to charge up yer phone

Way beyond my comfort zone

Too far away, too f*ckin' grim

Don't make me go to Tubuktim

The Issues in Devizes Poetry Slam

Well, toss me off with a trochee

And tickle me spondees as well

If it isn't The Issues Poetry Slam

And it seems that the buggers can spell

I spy some spectacular dactyls

And a neat bit o' wit and some verve

The odd limerick that is totally sick

And some shit kickin' humorous nerve

One's a beater of metre oneself, as you know

For by rhythm one's shaken and stirred

But sometimes free verse can take one from behind

With a bloody good earth shaking word

Choose humour! Choose life! Take a chance! Pen a rhyme!

Look in to form, or just wing it

Write the pain of your heart, tell the tale of a fart

Do what you like, but just bring it

Scat Magician

You're a sorcerer
Of course you are
You're darker than the night
You've brought out a book
I've just had a look
It's all about Satan
And shite

Your scat happy magic
Is weird and tragic
Ill wishing folk, really? How sad
Cursing with words
About cancer and turds
Not funny, not clever
Just bad

Those casting aspersions
On your Amazon versions
Will be turned in to piles of poo?
What is that smell
Someone's burning in hell
I reckon, you tosser
It's you

Told You So

On the Rocks

The Gift of Eros

Seven Year Itch

Told You So

wild winds

Cruel Wind

Pain and Ashes

Love and the Art of Motorcycle Maintenance

You're Not All That

Blistered

oubliette

The One

The Hate He Felt For Me

On The Rocks

Out on The Worms Head the birds screech and the sky wheels. She had fretted overnight about the tides, the window within which the journey could be made without drowning. She had seen an image of herself, fallen in the water, floating on the sea with heavy coat fanning out around her on the swell. He, having a far more cavalier approach to danger, lost patience early on and strode and clambered far ahead, becoming tiny and eventually lost to sight.

She became afraid. The rocks were jagged, slippy, hard to navigate. She became annoyed; all thoughts of independence flew away. He's left me and it serves me right. He's reckless, personality disordered and he doesn't give a damn. My love of him has brought me here and I may die upon the rocks. She catches up with him. He smiles and says "Well done" and opens up the flask. Resentment burns within her. He comments flippantly about the risk and she breaks. "I get what I deserve" she says "never wise to do dangerous stuff with psychopaths".

There is a momentary lull in the waves and the birds fall silent and drop from sight. His smile becomes a shadow. "I think we're done" he says and turns for the shore, a hint of a tear glinting in the shifting light. In that one moment she regrets; her amateur analysis, her arrogant assessment of her lover's soul, her words.

He strides for home and she stays motionless on the rocks.

The tide turns.

The Gift of Eros

Aloft flies Eros; mischief fluttered wings

With silent rustle whisper overhead

By arrows pierced; the hearts of knaves and kings

The chilly grave, the restless lover's bed

Blue London air, red Piccadilly light

Above the shifting crowd and constant noise

In summer heat, in neon and the night

He aims his slender bow with perfect poise

Aloft flies Eros; underneath his feet

As shadows of the Circus slowly shift

I contemplate my own love, bitter, sweet

The wound that Eros wrought in me, the gift

And as I turn my tears up to the sky

A pigeon drops an arrow in my eye

Seven Year Itch

your seven year itch;
flare of eczema infected
raw sore and weeping

your shattered hour glass;
irritating grains of sand
debriding old skin

your fingernail scratch;
sacrificial blood letting
scarification

your allergic rash;
self-fulfilling prophecy
psycho somatic

my fragility;
remedied with wisdom's balm
time passing quietly

Told You So

He said that he was broken

She told him she was broke

Neither took much notice

When the other person spoke

Far too bloody much in love

To weigh the implications

Not much need to forecast then

Future complications

She rationalised the broken thing

He thought that she would change

He thought she would make money

She thought he'd be less strange

You're not broken, love, she said

And chose a metaphor

You function on most channels

Just not on Radio 4

She's pretty good in bed, he thought

She's bright and going far

Shame she's getting on a bit

And hasn't got a car

The years went by so quickly

She watched him getting odd

Sometimes he was wonderful

Sometimes a total sod

She had to use a dictionary

To study mental health

He watched with disappointment

Her indifference to wealth

I told you so, he said, and she

Said she had told him too

And both of them remembered

What they had forgot they knew

He really was an odd one

And she didn't have a dime

And nowt would ever change those things

Not age nor luck nor time

There's nothing here for me, he thought

Her interest rate is falling

She's still in social housing

And her prospects are appalling

Love moves mountains, so she thought

I love him sane or mad

She thought that he still loved her too

She really had it bad

In the final conversation

They reviewed the words they'd spoken

How she had told him she was broke

And he said he was broken

I still love you so, she said

He shrugged, his eyes grew dim

With all the faith she had in love

She said these words to him

Take me, love, or leave me

For I always shall be poor

At that the bugger got his coat

And walked right out the door

wild winds

will he be
lost to the wild winds
or just
to me

Cruel Wind

Though safe from the wild winds

My love may be

It was a shivering

Cruel wind

That blew him back to me

No shelter from the storm

In him I see

Just unkind darkness

And no sanctuary

Pain and Ashes

Oh, speak to me of love, said Pain, now come
Draw up a chair and look me in the eye
Her limbs move slow, by sorrow frozen, numb
All nerve and sinew wracked by silent cry
Sit down, said Pain, the fire is hot and bright
And we must talk, for you have much to say
Not now, she begged, have mercy, not this night
Please let me speak of love another day
She feels the fire's scorch upon her face
As devastation sears and burns within
You must speak now, said Pain, there is no place
Nor corner left to hide in; so begin...
She sits in silence as the fire flashes
Till morning finds her, sat with Pain, and ashes

Love and the Art of Motorcycle Maintenance

Cold and careful hands
Dismantle love's elements
Methodically

The eye detecting
Fragile fractured copper threads
Dispassionately

Concentrating fire
Melting metal, soldered wire
Mending circuitry

Testing, one, two, three
The current, interrupted
Now set flowing free

How beautifully
Cool flux and hot flame restore
Conductivity

Love's analogy
Motorcycle maintenance
Electricity

You're Not All That

So I'm not looking good, you say

From where you are sat

Well, let me tell you, sonny Jim

You're not all that

I haven't quite lived up to your

Lofty aspirations

A bit too old, a bit too poor

Too many affectations

Incapable, impoverished

And just a bit autistic

Not even slightly racist

Or amusingly sadistic

You say I'm sadly lacking

Say it's sad perhaps, but true

That I'm no longer good enough

Not good enough for you

An eye for an eye, methinks

A tooth for a tooth

Would deem it fair enough that I

Should now tell the truth

That I should air our dirty laundry

On the corner of the street

And vomit dark unpleasantries

In puddles at your feet

Tell everybody everything

You've ever said to me

Let the fly on the wall that saw it all

Shout from the highest tree

But I shall never stoop so low

To where you are sat

For let me tell you, sonny Jim

You're not all that

Blistered

Grey days of loss and loneliness are here
Sad nights as long as shadows in the deep
No joy, no hope, no gentleness, no sleep
No ray of light predicted to appear
Just disappointment, emptiness, and fear
And sacred dreams discarded in a heap
By some abyss of faith too wide to leap
In ruins lies the love we held so dear

Wise folk will say there will be love again
That suns come up, and suns go down, and yet
All I perceive is darkness, drear and grim
All I can feel is searing hurt and pain
My heart, my fingers, too burnt to forget
All blistered, from the flame I hold for him

oubliette

from the oubliette

far down in the lonely ground

the sound of weeping

out of sight, but not of mind

drown out the echoes with wine

The One

He was The One, The One, The One

He was The One, it was true

And it would have been perfect, but for the fact

That he wasn't just one, he was two

It was just like a threesome, most of the time

There was me, there was Jekyll, and Hyde

Jekyll was honest, and loving, and kind

But Hyde had the devil inside

A turn of a sixpence, a phase of the moon

Imperceptible shifts of the light

And dear Mr Jekyll would turn in to Hyde

Who was darker than graves in the night

I just wanted Jekyll, just Jekyll, you see

But Hyde came as part of the deal

The addition of me, making two in to three

Made a triangle spin like a wheel

It was my fault, all my fault, everything

According to Hyde, in his view

They'd be better without me, Jekyll agreed

So that's when the three became two

Good luck to the pair of you, Jekyll, and Hyde

As you skip arm in arm to the sun

Well suited, free, but quite useless for me

For neither of you were The One

The Hate He Felt For Me

If I had known that he cared not for me
I would have dropped him, like a burning stone
Too blinded I, by silly love, to see
The hatred that he bore me to the bone
If I had seen beyond his wit, and charm
I could have passed him by upon the street
Protected heart from hurt, and pride from harm
Refrained from falling, fawning, at his feet
I should have sensed the loathing in his touch
The cold resentment in his blood and bile
Too lost was I, in silly love, too much
To see the silent scorn behind his smile
Now he is gone, and I shall ever be
Astounded by the hate he felt for me

With Love

The Glory of my Daughter

Crazy Eyes plays the Biscuit Game; *lust, mixed messages, and biscuits*

United, Reformed; *for Martin and Jayne Glover*

You Go, Girl; *Susan's leaving poem*

Tank Fest Tanka; *Tim Shaw goes to the Bovington Tank Festival*

Helmut Barlow; *Tim poses with Germans at the Bovington Tank Festival*

Catabolic Grace; *for Oliver Freeman, artist*

Transient Flame; *for Steve Herries*

Fickle Finger; *for Chris Greenwood*

Rockin' like Matthew Underwood

Cheeky Monkey; for Anne Rees

Serving the Grail; for Brad Combs; *Brad is the admin of The Writers Group on Facebook*

Dear Old Johnny Walter; *for my friend John*

Here Speaks the Magic Work of Raymond John; *for Raymond John Burt, author and poet*

Half a Century of Steve; *for Steve Bailey*

Karen's Keria; *for Karen Drabble*

The Birthday Rhyme That Never Was; *for Andy Fawthrop, poet*

Days of Wine and Blocked Noses

The Tantalisation of John Bruce

Tankfrotting; for Tim; *Tim's birthday*

Anna's Owl; *an owl lands on Anna Boulding's windowsill on her birthday*

The Glory of My Daughter

My daughter has come of age
Her name was in my heart and hand
All ready for her when my son was born
She does not look like me, having
Her father's face, his hair, his rare and angry flash
She studies hard, she sings
Like all the kinds of bird that sunlight wakens
Before she went away to learn her craft
She crept as silent as a mouse through life
Full of quiet apology, to men, to me
I nearly broke her, being careless, self-obsessed and unaware
Of her sweet spirit and her subtle energy
She left for university, with washing that she had to do herself

My daughter is a force majeure
She blasts on to the stage and brings
Her talent to the world
And she apologises less
She won't see victims shamed for their undress
She loves her friends and she loves me
She loves her brother, unsubserviently
My daughter wields a woman's power
My daughter bloometh like a flower
I never saw her beauty and to her face I called her
Like me, plain

In the last show I saw her play there was a Moment when
She hit a note, and let fall loose
Her mousey blonde yet glorious hair
I saw the glory of my daughter there

Crazy Eyes Plays the Biscuit Game

From the moment she looked at him, eyes all a-flutter
His shortbread was baked, with lashings of butter
As she pouted and simpered, her eyes all a-dreamy
His brain turned to custard, all sugared and creamy
Do have a biscuit, she offered one day
So he reached out his hand...and...
She pulled it away!

A few days later she produced a whole tin
Some with white icing and nutty bits in
The square ones looked good and the jammy ones dodgy
Enough to make several small children podgy
Help yourself, she said, as she offered him ten
So he reached out his hand...and...
She did it again!

Somewhat famished he found the game hard to digest
He quite fancied a biscuit, liked chocolate ones best
Something with fruit or an interesting crunch
Was surely one day on the menu for lunch
No really, she smiled, I've got one for you
So he reached out his hand...and...
Again she withdrew!

One time was funny, twice was unkind
By the third time the poor lad was out of his mind
In his dreams there were Jaffas and wafers all pinky
Luxurious wrappers and shapes that were kinky
He started to feel like a bit of a state
She tried it again...and...
He turned down the bait!

So, the end of the tale and this biscuit game ballad...

His appetite changed and he sought out some salad

No more was she able to hobble his knob

The next time she came with a crumb for his gob

He was wiser and said, You're a hot little piece

But you and your biscuits are...

Not very Nice!

United, Reformed

When the Queen of Sheba, so 'tis said
Came to ask of Solomon the King
Whether the tales told of him held true
He saw her beauty and entrusted her
With knowledge and the wisdom of all things

In this dear church today bedecked, with
Country flowers from Wiltshire gardens plucked
She comes to plight eternal troth to him
He stands beneath the Rood with certainty
The Rede she brings his true heart comprehends

In lilting voice the kind Welsh minister intones
A rare and ancient Scottish wedding rite
Rings grace their hands as tokens of their love
Engraven with the joy of Cornish lands
Solemn the vows they speak to man and God

Today so many complicated threads
Are bound together with simplicity
Two become one within the blesséd Trinity
Faith from the halls of history made new
United, reformed and sanctified with Love

You Go, Girl

Susan, dear Susanage, Sue
It's time for your Care Plan review
If delivering MOPSI
Has made you feel chopsy
You can fill in a feedback form too

Susan, dear Susanage, Sue
We're all very happy for you
You've scored one in the net
With a SMART goal and yet
Can you increase your eight points by two?

Susan, dear Susanage, Sue
A new risk assessment is due
There's a treatment break nigh
Your intensity's high
Best get a quick TOP out of you

Susan, dear Susanage, Sue
You've been brave and outspoken and true
And thoughtful and kind
Showing fullness of mind
In all that you think, say and do

Susan, dear Susanage, Sue
Off you tread on a highway that's new
You'll be Bad Ass in ways
Till the end of your days
You Go, Girl, with love from the crew

Tank Fest Tanka

baking in hot sun
spud boy wargasms like blitzkrieg
contemplating tanks

injustice of war ice cream
chocolate shrapnel sprinkled

Helmut Barlow

Tanked up in a tank top singing German boy band pop

The fame of Helmut Barlow has gone right over the top

His last track rolled to number two and could cause sleepless nights

Just one ferret in your turret and he'll have you in his sights

He'll straife you with his armoury and fire his weapon fast!

Military hard core! What a turn on! What a blast!

Catabolic Grace

land undulating
in to rolling furrows ploughed
defiant decay
waste of catabolic grace
dross in to gold in to dross

at the seasons edge
green waves, shining muddy rills
euphoric rising
flower painted battlefields
gold in to dross in to gold

Transient Flame

How time flies;
Like birds and bees
Transient nectar
Deciduous trees

How leaves fall;
Like stars in sky
Meandering streams
Passers by

How oceans flow;
Like blood in veins
Wind over mountains
Bloom strewn plains

How life flames;
Like a fire fly
Light in the shadows
New born cry

Fickle Finger

Sometimes, mate

The finger of fate

Uncomfortable, maybe

And fickle

May deliver a blow

But it's better, you know

Than the tickle

That comes

From a sickle

All shall be well

And all shall be well

All manner of things

Are intended

So contemplate this

As they're taking the piss

Sometimes fate

Is a mate

To be friended

Rockin' like Matthew Underwood

Another year, another candle

Lots of beer, a little scandal

Another wrinkle, more stuff learnt

More wisdom and more fingers burnt

We're here because we're here because

There's stuff to come and stuff that was

And we of the old school are still doin' good

Rockin' like Matthew Underwood

Cheeky Monkey; for Anne Rees

Anne is kind, she's fun, she's funky

Wears her colours strong and bright

What a cheeky little monkey

What a butterfly's delight

Serving the Grail; for Brad Combs

A kindly sword and savage pen
Are the marks of a writer and leader of men
Blessed be he who came to teach
The wildness of wisdom and freedom of speech
Where fainter hearts might fall and fail
He stands to serve the Writer's Grail
This ancient sage; this humble youth
This herder of cats; this teller of truth
Is he we know and love as Brad
Our literary Galahad

Dear Old Johnny Walter

Here comes Johnny Walter, the old geezer on the bike

When he waves and says "Hello there" there's not much not to like

He is kind and he is funny, and he's full of Wiltshire wit

He remembers everybody's name and gets about a bit

For a man of nearly eighty his humour is quite dry

Never underestimate the twinkle in his eye

A Moonraker, a character, an ancient Briton, he

Who reckons that his ancestors lived in Avebury

A child of New Park Street, who heard and smelled and saw

The weary trains of soldiers marching homewards from the war

Who, when he was a teenager, learned how to spin a spool

And hung out at The Palace, and was far too cool for school

Imagine all the movies that he showed throughout the years

How he moved an auditorium to laughter, shock and tears

Fifty years of pictures, all those newsreels and Bond

Folk walking home from Psycho, getting spooked out by the pond

Folk snogging in the back row, swapping hormones, spit and smoke

The porn, the pot, the popcorn, and the icecream, and the coke

Johnny hung out with the Mods and took a scooter trip to France

And liked to watch the ladies, with a beer, at a dance

Until he married Margaret; 'twas as his father said

"If you take her to the bedroom, you will end up in the bed"

Johnny didn't mind at all when she with child fell

First came little baby Michael, and then Carolyn as well

And the cottage, out in Cheverell, where flowed a little stream

Happy years of family, a rural rosy dream

Until the day that Margaret was taken far too soon

Leaving Johnny on his own, to marvel at the chilly moon

He kept calm, and carried on, 'cos he's a solid sort of guy

Kids to bring up, work to do and not much time to cry

But to this day he misses her, puts flowers on her grave

One could call him stoical, or practical, or brave

Yet in his quiet moments, sometimes, silent tears fall

Better to have loved, he thinks, than not have loved at all

Kept calm and carried on, and bore his lot with love and grace

Always greeting friends with a bright smile on his face

He stirred the jam at Easterton, rang all the village bells

He filled the air with music and with sweetened fruity smells

He's still batty in a belfry, still a jammy sort of cove

You'll see him with his faithful dog, with whom he likes to rove

You might think he's a boy racer, in his go fast stripey car

He knows who's who, and who does what, and where wild flowers are

He has grandchildren, great grandchildren, a garden, and some fish

He has the sort of life for which most decent folk would wish

He is full of Wiltshire wisdom, in a quiet sort of way

You'll see him thinking carefully about what he should say

When he meets you in the street, and doffs his syrup and his hat

And asks after your family, your garden, and your cat

He has some little sayings, gleaned from years of Wiltshire lore

But doesn't always understand what certain words are for

He can sometimes drop a clanger, with no malice or intent

And once he even asked me what 'bisexual' meant

"We're all different" he says, "it just don't do to be the same

Tubs should rest on their own bottoms, for the best chance at the game"

He is a loyal friend to many, and a much belovéd Dad

Just the kindest lovely man that Wiltshire ever had

'Tis true that good things come in some unusual disguises

Like dear old Johnny Walter, gentle spirit of Devizes

Here Speaks The Magic Work Of Raymond John

Here speaks the magic work of Raymond John
Intriguing reference, enlightened phrase
I'm curious as to what, my friend, you're on
That powers your pen to so the mind amaze
Let he that has an ear be still and hear
Let she who has an eye seek out the light
For here some crazy wisdom doth appear
On wild wings of angels in the night
For Love and God and Death and Grace and Hell
Within your words take buttered toast and tea
More syllabub, Beelzebub? Pray tell
What syllables might set the Sibyls free
Get thee behind me, ghosts, take flight, be gone!
Here speaks the magic work of Raymond John

Steve, mate, I can't come tonight
Public transport's total shite
Trains and buses, Trowbridge, Bath
The station down some dodgy path
So I'm just going to drop a rhyme
And hope you have a bangin' time...

Half A Century of Steve

Fifty, Steve! That's five times ten
Years you'll not get back again
I hear your voice speak in my ear
How the fuck did I get here?
Mate, fifty years of learning stuff
Have made you kind, and wise, and tough
Fair play, you've had your ups and downs
But all of us be saints, and clowns

You've lived your life with throttle up
Found many cups from which to sup
Been serious, enjoyed a joke
Passed wisdom on to other folk
You've carpe'd diem, seized the day
You've sped along the motorway
Done stuff with metal I don't get
Kept powder dry and solder wet

A tinker with a massive bike
A bloke who isn't hard to like
Who knows that real men sometimes cry
(Is that a twinkle in your eye?)
You see the rainbow in the rain
And, when you fall, get up again
Let's face it, it takes quite a man
To be a match for our Leanne

So, Steve, mate; love and all the best
Sink ten for me and then the rest
Dance like no-one's watching, then
Have more beer and dance again
But one more thing before I go
For this I'd quite like you to know...

Whatever forces gave you birth
Sure put some precious salt on earth

Karen's Keria

Karen lovely Keria

Is like the sun, but yellower

Apparently the moniker

Means Japanese Japonica

Karen's lovely Keria

Is like the sun, but mellower

Such blooms to make a geisha sing

Are quite

A haiku

Sort of

Thing

The Birthday Rhyme That Never Was

What are words that rhyme with Andy?

Handy, bandy, Gandhi, randy?

Fawthrop? F*ck all rhymes with that

At least not from where I am sat

Fair cop, Fawthrop, could be worse

I started writing you a verse

That mentions 'sop', 'slop', 'pop', and 'flop'

But I quite like you, so I'll stop

Days Of Wine And Blocked Noses

Administering medication

Must needs be done in moderation

For wine was made to make men glad

Not maudlin and morose and sad

A tot of toddy may bring cheer

But not a Crammer full of beer

For spirits raised within a glass

Will fall as sure as night will pass

And a respiratory depressant

May well not quell a cough incessant

My patronising rant is flagging

You're reeling now from all the nagging

Just leave some in the bottle spare

Take water with it, and fresh air

The Tantalisation of John Bruce

Outside looking in

From John's pocket moths appear

As violins weep

Beggars from the pavement see

Art through a glass darkly

Grayson's woven tales

Of social mobility

Inaccessible

Myths of the tapestries lost

To legend and irony

Illicit colours

Seep through windows to the street

Teasing with beauty

Sweet tale of the poet's life

John Bruce; tantalised by light

Tankfrotting; for Tim

Tim, Tim
The skittish young buck
Still on the Viagra
And up for a ... *turn or two on the croquet lawn*

Tim, Tim
He gets younger each day
A little bit fatter
And slightly less gay

Tim, Tim
Likes to frot the odd tank
At the whim of the wind
He can whip up a ... *rather fine champagne cocktail*

Tim, Tim
So complex, yet simple
Like unicorn porn
Or a gimp in a wimple

Tim, Tim
You playful young Puck
Keep on pulling yer pork
Yer as funny as ... *more amuse bouche, vicar?*

Tim, Tim
May your light never dim
And the sun always shine
On the edge of your rim

Anna's Owl

A sudden owl
Too wit too woo
A window sill
Too woo too wit
A message of
True wit to you
A sacred gift
To you true wit
A mystic sign
An owl, and you
Two wise old birds
Too wit too woo

Two Short Stories

Martha and the Doll

Skank

Martha and the Doll

It's a particularly dull day for photographs. The light is poor and there is an irritating drizzle in the air. Folk have stayed at home or are venturing, with heavy reluctance, only as far as their shopping needs dictate. It's February; a month of meagre pickings, low in inspiration, high in desperation, and one winter month more than most folk can stand. These are days for antidepressants and undertakers, days of whining and blocked noses, days to be slept through, suffered, survived. It's a beige and grey sort of day, in which colours struggle to vibrate and not much contrasts much with anything, the sort of day when litter looks interesting in a desert of gloom. February. Not a month for images to amaze the eye.

Martha treads the dreary ways of town with quiet and humble feet. She wears her sorrows round her shoulders in black bedraggled imitation fur, and between her naked sandalled toes in grimy crevices. Old and free, of teeth, of obligation, she shuffles the streets, as she used to do when she did not have a home, as she has always done. Martha likes to think outside the box. Indoors she is unhappy, restless, lonely; a fish out of water, deprived of life. Walls stifle and depress her. Surfaces demand cleaning. People want to come round and mend things. Windows blur the beauty of the sky. There is no air, and worrying things in envelopes insist themselves, clattering, through her door. Martha's sorrows, the tales of which are for another time, or maybe never, are more than many folk could bear, yet still she walks, as if there were somewhere to go, somewhere perhaps where there may still be joy to be found.

What Martha likes, more than ordinary things, more than money or appearances, what Martha cares about the most, is animals. She sends money to donkeys in distant lands, and prays for them. She goes to church at Christmas to see the Nativity donkey, and strokes him with the same gentleness and innocence that children show to little things. You will see her standing by the bridge sometimes, watching the ducks, peering through the chicken wire at the merry hens running free in the field by the graveyard. Sometimes there are horses there, and honking geese. Many chilly hours will pass as Martha stands observing the animals and the chattering, flapping, friendly birds, wondering if they have enough to eat, wondering whether they are warm enough. The ghost of her faithful, long dead, long-suffering dog walks along with her wherever she wanders, adhered to her ankles for always. Stay, she had said, and so he did.

She is sitting on the top of the litter bin without a coat, her little toes all rosy in the air, dressed for summer in tomboy tee shirt and trousers. Her eyes are blue and her lips are pink. She has mischievous strands of blonde escaping messily from her long pigtails. She's pretty, and poignant, and lost. The photographer, grateful for the surprise of an interesting subject, stops at this oasis of visual delight to drink. Snap, one with the doll and the bin and the bars of the Shambles gate, one close up, one further away, one portrait shot and three for luck, quickly, before some crying child returns to snatch up the doll and cuddle her close.

The photographer was never one for toys, or plastic, or cute things. This doll, though, she's kind of special. There is some glint of humour in her almost human expression and the hint of a smile on her mouth. Across her chubby pink cheeks flicks the nuance of a personality. She has a lovely face. Someone will miss her, thinks the photographer, putting her satisfied camera in her pocket. After a brief moment of hesitation, during which she contemplates adoption, she leaves the little doll on the litter bin to be found.

There is not much left to do in town. What scant light exists within this ordinary day is dimming fast. The photographer wanders aimlessly for a while, buying cigarettes and lipstick and cleaning things that she will never use. She looks forward to going home and playing with the photos of the doll on her computer. Perhaps I will post a picture on the internet, she thinks, and see if anyone knows who the doll belongs to, thereby satisfying my own ego and the purposes of altruism in one artistic act. Not that I'm pretentious or anything. Much. Mostly. Maybe. But then what use would my picture be if the doll has gone? She wished that she had picked her up now, and handed her in to the police station or the library. Someone might just throw the little doll away. Or she might get hypothermia from sitting on the bin all night. Or someone really mean might take her home. The delight she gleaned from capturing the image of the doll fades as she ruminates, and she regrets deciding against rescuing the doll. She feels guilty, as she did when she was young and less than kind to teddies. She wanders in to Smiths to see if the purchase of an unnecessary object will afford any comfort from her nagging conscience.

"Oh," she says, smiling "you picked her up then!" For there, by the magazines, is Martha, and there, in Martha's gentle hands, is the doll. "What do you mean?" says Martha, looking worried as if she might be in some sort of trouble. "The little doll, I've just taken some pictures of her." "Have you, can I look?" The photographer shows her the pictures in her camera. Martha looks at them with fascination, as if they were magic. "Such a shame," says Martha "someone just left her there, all by herself." She shows the photographer the doll's tiny bare toes, stroking them to warm them up. "And she has no shoes on, all on her own in the cold with no shoes or coat, not nice for her at all." "Someone must have lost her." "No, I don't think so, she's been in a sale." She points out a paper tag in the doll's dishevelled hair, on which '£3' is faintly scrawled. "She has alopecia" remarks the photographer, flippantly, regretting the comment immediately. "She's got what?" says Martha, whose wisdom does not lie in words. "It means that she has a bit of hair loss. What are you going to do with her?" "I'm going to take her home and look after her. Poor little thing, all lost and lonely and cold. It's not fair, it's not fair at all. She needs to be in the warm, all warm and safe, with new clothes and shoes and her hair brushed. She's a lovely little thing. It's not fair on her. Fancy someone just leaving her like that. On a bin, like rubbish. It's not right, not right at all." "What are you going to call her?" Martha thinks carefully. "I don't know." She holds the doll tight to her chest. It doesn't seem to mind the bedraggled coat at all. It even seems, although it must be a trick of the artificial light, to smile. "I hope she'll be happy with you, Martha" says the photographer, and goes down the aisle in search of superfluous pens. From the end of the shop she can hear Martha talking to the shop assistant "Have you got a carrier bag that I can put her in, no, not that one, that's too small, she won't be comfortable, do you have a bigger one, yes, that will do, she'll fit nicely in that one, thank you, thank you very much."

It is a week or two before the photographer sees Martha again. Hours spent trying to edit the photographs had not been well spent. Somehow, with all the tweaking of contrast and clarity possible, she had not been able to do the doll justice with her editing programme. The image sits in her computer, waiting patiently to be perfected. Martha is in Smiths again, without the doll but with cheerful bright eyes, freshly washed hair and her best earrings on. "How are you, Martha, and how is the doll?" "Oh, she's very well," says Martha, smiling, "she's sitting on the settee at home. She's warmer now, poor pretty little thing, it wasn't right you know." "I'm glad," says the photographer "I wanted to ask you, I wonder if you would you mind if I wrote about it, you know, you and the doll, just a little piece to go with the photograph, I can change your name if you like?" Martha looked thoughtful. "And what would you do with it?" "I don't know yet, I haven't decided, but I thought it would be a nice thing to write about. Such a lovely doll." "Yes," said Martha "you write what you like. Poor little thing. No shoes on. Left out in the cold. Not fair. Not fair at all." And off walks Martha, with a spring in her step and the faithful ghost of her dog at her ankles, finally and unexpectedly finding herself with a good reason to go home.

Skank

Skank polished her designer shades with her hoody and perched them on the end of her nose. She liked her shades, partly because they were cool and partly because she could study passers-by intently and without fear of recrimination. The first afternoon of autumn was quiet and the streets bereft; with summer and carnival receding in memory and disappearing from timelines folk were left with empty pockets and looming anxieties about when to put on the heating and how to cope with the slow fall to Christmas. Skank had stale air and holes in her pockets, and a silent scream in her stomach and veins. She shifted on the bench and stroked her hair with her hand. She cared about her hair a lot. Come pain or moonshine she always had pretty hair, smoothed and shone and straightened, thick and glossed with many a stolen product.

No rick pickings today, she thought. Skank was new to the area and had a brief window of time to scam folk before she got a name for herself. It had gone well so far. She had a nose for them, bleeding hearts, and there seemed to be plenty of them in this town. She mainly went for middle aged women, teenagers and very old men. The middle aged women liked to feel charitable, the teenagers were easily intimidated and the old men were sentimental and embarrassingly grateful to be flattered by a young girl. Skank had an impressive repertoire of begging lines. She had used "Lost me purse and have to get back to Bath" on a non-existent bus on thirty occasions, had needed "Money for the phone to ring up someone to bring me epilepsy medication in to town" eleven times, had "Run out of dog food" for an invisible hound thirteen times, had to "Go to court in Swindon" four times, needed to "Visit a dying relative in Melksham" frequently and had produced "Embarrassed to mention it but require emergency sanitary protection with immediate effect" seven times. Then there was the straightforward "Starving, haven't eaten for a week" the brazen, "Give us a quid I'll give it back to you when I get me giro, honest, swear on me kids' lives" and the killer, "Got to get back to the kids with some tea" lines. The last one worked best. She also found that a sycophantic "God bless your heart" finished off most interactions nicely.

Most days the lines went well, the hair stayed straight and the pockets filled but on other days it rained, the hair frizzed and, tiresomely, people tried to help her. They rang hostels, they bought her food she would never eat, they offered her sleeping bags and moral support, they offered to take her to the council and the food bank and gave her good advice that she had heard so often it just slipped off her brain. Old ladies promised to pray for her and old gentlemen were eager to install her on their sofas for a price. I only want an effing quid, she would think to herself, smiling and nodding behind her shades and making the odd grateful noise, keep your effing do-good sh*te to yourself and just give me the wonga. In her mind it was simple, I want money, you've got money, give me some of your money and don't waste my time. But, to her endless frustration, the people she picked out always wanted more from the interaction. They wanted validation. That they were good, or cool, or more charitable than the next man, or destined for heaven, or something special, or more possessed of tolerance than the average, or richer, or more effective, or wiser than most. Skank could smell this need around a person. It was her way in to their hearts and wallets. Just a shame that it was so time consuming.

She'd had some gear that morning but the effects were wearing off now and she could feel the sickness coming. Shifty was at home in bed, incapable of anything much but the odd punch and some verbal abuse. She didn't know if she loved Shifty. They had moved here to make a new start but had brought themselves with them, and it had not taken long for them to be subsumed in to local using circles and to replicate their old life. Shifty was in and out of prison, hard as nails and quickly establishing himself as the main man. He had filled the void left by the last one, who had finally been put down for a decent stretch, much to the relief of local shopkeepers and the constabulary. Nature abhors a vacuum and Shifty had stepped in to Tyrone's shoes faster than a blink. She was with him because, because, because he had a fast ass, because he was a habit, because he was hard and because he would not let her go. She had twice his brains but he hit the hardest. They had been together since she was fourteen. They had a child when she was fifteen, a little boy whom she had called Alfie after her grandad. Alfie had been removed from her arms in the hospital. He had screamed and she had cried. Alfie was now with some strange happy family somewhere else. He had survived heroin withdrawal at birth and was now a recovering addict, aged three.

Skank had found that heroin helped her to forget about Alfie. Heroin helped her to forget what feeling was altogether. With heroin she was invisible, invincible, floating in a sensory deprivation tank, bathed in warm cotton wool and custard, beautiful, immune. She had never quite been able to replicate the bliss of her first hit, well the third. The first two times she had retched and gone in and out of consciousness and thought she might die. The third time the spot was hit and as she went on the nod she dreamed of heaven and her flesh became infused with glory. From that moment on hitting the spot became a devastating obsession, more important than Alfie, or Shifty, or pride, or reputation, or self-respect. More important than food or love or the future and almost more important than her hair. She had tried, once, to stop using. There had been a drought and Shifty had been doing time for mugging an old lady. She had hassled the doctor for codeine and he had referred her to drug services. She was fine on the methadone for a while, despite the fact that it was crashingly dull, and had started to reduce her dose and not use on top. Then Shifty came out of prison and beat her up and it all began to seem pointless and she gave up giving up. When he started pimping her out she started to need a lot more heroin and began to turn tricks behind his back, always looking over her shoulder, always looking over punters' shoulders, in case he appeared to claim his own.

The other thing that heroin helped Skank to forget was her childhood. Her parents had taught her violence, swearing, poverty, conflict, dishonesty and fear. They had used her as a pawn in their mind games, as whipping boy and scapegoat, as a passport to benefits and housing, as cleaner, cook, carer and courier. They had filled her pushchair with stolen meat and alcohol and sent her out begging in the cold with holes in her shoes. She had had so many fathers that they all merged in to one and she categorised them in to the ones that touched her up, the ones that hit her and the ones that did both. She had craved her mother's love but had been passed over time and time again for each new hero of the house. In the end she grew cold and silent and withdrew to her tiny cupboard bedroom to play with her hair and self-harm. She was careful to cut in places that no-one would see. The surface of her skin became in time a landscape of abuse, all lakes of bruises and ridges of scars, an undergarment of livid despair. The last straw, the final insult, came on the day when the latest squeeze invited his friends round when her Mum was out nicking. All was fine to start with but as the empty whisky bottles began to populate the living room floor and the shouting got louder and glasses were broken Skank became afraid and locked herself in her room. She shook in fear as she heard stumbling and laughter on the stairs. Then they started banging on the door. "Come out and play, you little whore, you're Mum's a right goer and the apple don't fall far from the tree" "Go away, leave me alone" said Skank. This enraged them and they banged harder and louder until the door broke. They pulled Skank out of the tiny room and raped her on the landing, laughing. Then they took her downstairs and raped her again, in more adventurous ways. Then they went to the pub. When her Mum got home she was rocking on the floor half naked and bleeding. "What the f**k have you been up to?" Asked Mum "Where's my man?" Skank tried to tell her, she cried and pressed herself to her mother's breast, desperate to be held and believed and saved "You little bitch," said her Mum, "get out of my house!" She thumped her hard on the way out of the door and Skank never went home again.

Skank snuffled and fidgeted on the benches by the old Post Office, waiting for an unsuspecting ship to come in, becoming achey and sweaty and just a little desperate. Other users came and went, with bags of stolen meat and bottles of sherry and unlikely business propositions regarding half a bag of gear next Jalloon and complaints about the unfairness of life. Someone had some dog ends and Skank accepted a puff. She wanted them all to go away. No one would give her money if she was sat with that lot. She liked a couple of them but in this game it was every man for himself. Keep your friends close and your dealer closer. Trust no-one and no-one can betray your trust. If you haven't got a granny you can sell for a tenner then sell someone else's. And don't grass unless it pays well. These were the rules. People moved swiftly on when they realised that Skank was not in for going in on any mythical deals and soon she was alone again. She wasn't a paranoid person but it became immediately evident that there was something different going on today. A couple of people crossed the street without saying hello. A stranger scowled at her with peculiar intensity. One of the ladies who had helped her out more than once would not catch her eye on passing, becoming abnormally engrossed with her phone. A couple of teenage boys pointed at her and laughed. A young Mum seemed very concerned with pulling her children away from the benches. And someone let their poodle piss right next to her. Skank became uneasy. Last week she had tapped someone up for a quid and the interaction had been unusually intense. She had chosen the combination of "Bus to Bath" "Hungry children" "Lost me purse" and "Swear on me kids' lives" on this woman. It hadn't gone down well. The woman said that she had heard it all before and had looked Skank in the eye with a burning gaze and asked her straight if she would be spending the money on drugs. Skank had held her gaze with an eyelid flicker barely perceptible to the naked eye and lied through her teeth. The woman had asked what time the bus left and Skank had told another lie. The woman had given her the pound. To the statement "God bless your heart" she had replied that if she found out Skank was scamming her she would hunt her down. These chilling words had been delivered with a comedy voice and a penetrating stare. Since that day Skank had slipped in to the shadows when she saw the woman but the woman's stare followed her every time.

On the day that she was scammed by Skank, Brenda had simply had enough. Generally she was a soft touch, believing in the 'What goes around comes around pass it on do as you would be done by' way of going about things. She had helped people out on numerous occasions and was always good for a fag at least. But recently the constant requests for cash and assistance had worn holes in her charity and she had become weary of supporting people who seemed utterly disinclined to lift a finger for themselves. She was sick of the sob stories and no longer flush enough to subsidise others. She thought a lot about charity and its positive and negative consequences. She hated it when people slagged off the homeless and people on benefits. She had considerable sympathy with addiction and some relevant experience herself on both sides of treatment services. People had helped her out in the past. People had been tolerant and understanding and supported her through difficult times. Her heart went out to the people in the woods and the drinkers on the benches. She did what she could when she could in different ways, either helping people directly, or by signposting them to relevant agencies. She tried to give them unpatronising advice when advice was sought, and spoke up for them in hostile forums. She made a conscious effort to be kind and to treat everyone the same. She wasn't interested in reward. She just didn't want to be taken for a mug. But today, she really had had enough, and spoke to Skank in a way that surprised even her. As Skank slid away Brenda knew that she was stupid to have given the money. She had known Skank was lying but had been incapable in some way of saying no. She was angry with herself and angry with Skank. The bile of resentment rose within her and ruined her walk home. It was still with her the next day, along with a feeling of foolishness and betrayal, when she saw Skank hiding behind one of the users in town. So she went home, switched on her computer, plastered Skank's name all over the town websites and cranked up a virtual lynch mob.

In the space of an hour seventy people posted tales of their own experiences with Skank and her various scamming methods. A pattern emerged involving more travel to Bath than was humanly possible, along with tales of mythical hungry dogs and debilitating medical conditions, dying relatives in Melksham and lost purses. People were disappointed, surprised and annoyed that their well-meant charity had been so badly used. One young girl had been so intimidated that she had given Skank her lunch money on more than one occasion. One old lady reported that her purse had gone missing after a friendly chat. Several dog lovers had been taken in by the invisible hound story. More than one respectable middle aged lady had been moved to tears and donation by the tale of the hypothetical children. And several blokes were offering to 'sort her out'. The voices of those advising tolerance and understanding were drowned out by the shouts of those baying for blood. Brenda's schadenfreude was short lived. The satisfaction her vengeful act accorded her lasted precisely seven minutes, by which point she had whipped up a dangerous storm. She had no-one to blame but herself. The voice of her conscience screamed in her ear and her bleeding heart sank like a stone. It was a long time since Brenda had done anything truly sh*tty but she had excelled herself with this one. Skank at least had a powerful addiction to excuse her. Brenda had no excuse. She should have known better and she knew it. She had 'acted out' on her emotions. She had fanned the flames of ignorance and hatred with her own hand. And all for the sake of a pound. Overwhelmed by shame Brenda went to bed early and tried to hide under her pillow. From herself.

Skank's need for heroin was increasing. Her choices were to either beg and scam or steal and fence, or go home to the abusive Shifty and spend three or four horrible nights in a psychological and physical hell. She hated being sick with Shifty. He would cry and moan and sweat and toss and turn and make everything her fault, adding insult after insult to self-induced injury, aiming the odd feeble punch at her for refusing to go in to town and turn tricks. She liked to grit her teeth when she was sick, and lie as still and silent as possible. The third night was always the worst, if you could get through that you were home free. Only that would always, like New Year's Day, be the time when the man would knock at the door with the world's smallest bag. And they would fall on him with fawning gratitude rather than leap the hurdle of one more endless night. Sharing a habit was a problem doubled. They never wanted to stop using at the same time and constantly sabotaged each other, time and time again. She had to get some gear. The alternative was unthinkable. She picked her target and fired her shaggy dog food story at the most likely candidate. But the lady with the particularly ugly pug gave her short shrift. "You don't have a dog," she said "don't ask me again" The pug smirked in the full knowledge of a forthcoming luxury tea and proceeded to defecate in front of Poundland. "My Mum says I'm not to give you any money," said a teenage girl with uncharacteristic confidence, "go away!" "You're having a laugh, aren't you?" said a cheerful builder, "Piss off" And finally, "F**k off, skanky bitch," from a shaven headed lad, "you ripped off my Nan" which statement was followed by a hefty right hook. Skank reeled with pain and bewilderment. The only person who had hit her in this town to date was Shifty. It was the least violent place she had ever been. She was shocked and embarrassed. And her hair was a mess. She drew the line at crying in public, pulled up her hood, balanced her shades painfully on her nose and took herself to Gracie's house, dripping blood all down her clothes.

Skank almost loved Gracie. Gracie reminded her of her dead gran and had a kind and lovely soul. Her house smelled of lavender and baking and had a front room that nobody sat in, an outside loo and a small garden where cheerful gnomes conspired around a small pond. Gracie's long dead husband Ron had kept pigeons and the loft was still there, waiting for ghosts to fly home. Gracie channelled a lot of love. She knew all about Skank and her habit. And she was the only person Skank ever spoke to about Alfie. One of the things Skank loved most about going to Gracie's house was that she didn't have to lie or pretend or be hard at all. Gracie accepted her with all her failings. Skank hated asking her for money. She would listen to Gracie talk and accept her offer of biscuits, all the while dreading the moment when she had to pop the question. Gracie only had her pension but she saw Skank as the child she had never had and was happy to share. "Oh dear," said Gracie "you are in the wars. Look at your hair. We'd better clean you up and you can tell me all about it" She ran Skank a bath and gave her a warm fluffy towel and a dressing gown. Skank looked at herself in the bathroom mirror. Her hair was caked in blood and her eye was swelling up. She took off her dirty clothes and looked at her whole body with its scars and bruises and prominent ribs and needle marks. This isn't OK, thought Skank, dismayed, this has to stop. As she sat in the bath enjoying the heat, wincing at the pain, feeling achier and sicker by the minute, she made a plan. Tomorrow she would go to the doctor and get referred back in to treatment. She would leave Shifty and start over. Tomorrow would be the first day of the rest of her life. She could go back to college, get a job, meet a decent guy and have a future. Skank was bright. Really bright. She would have done well as school had she been encouraged more, or had she had the kind of home life where one was fed and hugged and had a decent night's sleep in a warm bed. She had had to use her intelligence to merely survive. It wasn't too late. She was only eighteen. It could all change and all this chaos just become a memory of youthful folly. That was that then. She had decided. The quest for conditioner proved fruitless so she just combed her wet hair and made a mental note to nick some later, then remembered that it was all going to stop. Tomorrow. She put on the dressing gown and went to sit with Gracie in the kitchen. Her clothes were tumbling in the drier and the kitchen was warm with steamed up windows. There was a strangely comforting smell of washing powder and cabbage. "So, what happened?" asked Gracie. Skank told her about the pug lady and the punch. "Mmm," said Gracie "I need to show you something."

Gracie had been going to the library recently and had been learning about computers from teenage boys. She had found that she had quite a knack with them and had bought herself a laptop. Her learning curve had been steep and swift and she had mastered the dark arts of Facebook and Twitter, got back in touch with those friends from her childhood who were still alive and played Bridge regularly with her cousin in

Canada. She fired up the laptop. "You won't like this," she said "but you need to know" She went on to the most popular town Facebook page and passed the computer to Skank. Skank scrolled down past the requests for information about Poundland opening times and for advice on how to complete simple bodily functions and there it was. Brenda's vitriolic post. Followed by over two hundred comments, from people she had scammed mainly, and also some from people she had never met. A few voices spoke up for her, saying that she probably had issues and needed help, but most were angry and upset to realise that they were not the only people to have contributed to the wellbeing of the incorporeal dogs and theoretical children. Some even had some novel ideas regarding summary execution. All agreed that she had been Taking the P*ss. When she read the post from the autistic girl who had felt intimidated she almost agreed with them. "Who is Brenda?" she asked Gracie, as there was only an abstract photograph representing the architect of her ruination. When Gracie described Brenda the penny dropped. Skank knew that there had been something unusual about that interaction and had been dreading Brenda's revenge. And here it was. A new kind of violence with far reaching implications. It was only a pound, thought Skank, what a bitch. And yet everything that was said on the page regarding her own actions was true. Sh*t. "Gracie, what am I going to do?" she said, afraid, "They hate me" "That's not quite true, is it?" said Gracie "Some of them have been trying to help you. And even some of the people you have deceived are still speaking up for you. Perhaps if you had taken some of the help you have been offered you wouldn't be in this mess. Haven't you had enough yet?" Skank had a think. She had indeed had enough of her lifestyle, the endless round of scamming, scoring, shooting up, sleeping, waking up, getting sick and doing it all again. The adrenaline hit of shoplifting had worn thin and anyway she was banned from most of the shops in town. She hated turning tricks, satisfying seedy men who made her skin crawl, for a few poxy quid. She had certainly had enough of Shifty. But had she had enough of heroin? Of this she was unsure. Which was where a methadone script would come in handy. Whatever Russell Brand had to say on the matter. She had been to a Narcotics Anonymous meeting once. Lots of spiritual waffle mixed with a bit of bullshit. But the folk there had looked happy and did a lot of laughing. There was definitely something in it but she wasn't sure what. People had been friendly to her for no apparent reason and two women had given her their phone numbers. And then she had lifted someone's bag on the way out, which kind of sullied the experience and meant that she could not go back again. "I think I have had enough, Gracie," she said "but I am afraid" "What you need," said Gracie "is a bit of courage and determination. And a biscuit" She offered Skank a homemade cookie. It looked and smelt delicious but wasn't the sustenance Skank's body required right now. "Can I take some with me?" she asked as she dressed in warm clothes fresh from the tumble drier. "Of course," said Gracie and carefully wrapped four cookies in some greaseproof paper "here you go" Skank put them in her pocket, hugged Gracie and thanked her, and made for the front door. She very nearly managed to leave without asking for money but old habits die hard. As she opened the garden gate she turned and said "I don't suppose you could spare a tenner, Gracie, I'll give it back when I get me giro?" The internet had opened a whole new world to Gracie and she had been doing a lot of research about addiction in order to try and help Skank. "I'm not going to enable you anymore," she said "but you will always find a meal and a warm bed and a hug here. Remember I love you" Tears sprang to Skank's eyes. She got it. She ran back down the path, kissed Gracie without a word and then headed back to town.

Running the gauntlet of whispers and scowls in the town centre was an uncomfortable experience and Skank kept her head down. "Oi" said a familiar voice "Shifty's got some gear at yours, you'd best get home quick before he does it all" She broke in to a run. A little bit of gear was all she needed to give her the strength to get some food down her, to go to the doctor's, to leave Shifty and her awful life once and for all. It would stop all the pain and distress that consumed her and give her some breathing space. Her body yearned in anticipation. She flung open the front door of their tiny bedsit shouting "Shifty, save some for me!" There was no reply. Shifty was on the floor by the cooker in a strange position with a needle hanging out of his arm, barely breathing and turning blue. "Shifty!" She shook him and slapped him and took the pin out of his arm. A drop of spittle dropped from his mouth and he emitted a feeble groan. She reached for her phone. No credit. She reached for his phone. No credit. She banged on the neighbour's door. No answer. She picked up the remains of the heroin, put it in her pocket and ran out in to the street. She ran in to the nearest shop "Get out, you're banned" said the security guard "But my partner has just OD'd" she cried "please call an ambulance" "Yeah, right," said the guard, he didn't get where he was today by helping wasters "just f**k off" She ran to the benches where the users were sat "Shifty's gone over," she said in desperation "has anyone got a phone?" "Nah, no credit, he'll be alright, bloody good gear, mind" was the consensus, and then "Haven't you got a Naloxone pen?" Skank didn't even know what a Naloxone pen was but she knew she didn't have one. Then there was "Don't call the police, they'll nick you" and "Got any money on you?" Someone waved a bottle of sherry under her nose and she took a swig before she ran off to see if anyone else would be more helpful. "Pull the other one, it's got bells on" said one woman "Nah, you can't use my phone, you'll just run off with it" said another "You and that scumbag deserve all you get" was the view of several people and some little girls told her to do one. She ran to the Market Place, stood on the Market Cross and screamed "Please help me, Shifty is dying, I need to phone an ambulance, I don't want any money, I just need to make a phone call, for God's sake help me, please!" "Drunk again" said one office worker to another "Get away from my car" said a businessman "You're that girl that's always scamming people," said a war veteran "bring back National Service" "Got that tenner you owe me?" said the woman from the Market "F**k off you cow, get a life" said someone who had once been a punter, someone so revolting that she had actually refused his money in the end, leaving him with a grudge. "Please, please, Shifty is dying!" She pulled on peoples' coat sleeves, she cried and begged and pleaded, she ran in to the estate agents, the newsagents and the pub, but no-one would help her. She ran back to the bedsit, blinded by tears and sweat. In the twenty minutes she had been trying to get help Shifty had stopped breathing and died. She fell to her knees beside him and wailed with grief. She wailed for half an hour. Somewhere, as if from a long way off down a tunnel, came the sound of someone banging at a door.

In slow motion, Skank kissed Shifty's lifeless lips, injected the rest of the heroin, picked up the kitchen scissors, walked to the mirror and cut off all her hair.

***

The years had not been kind to Brenda. She had heard all about Shifty's death, through the town websites, in the papers and on the street. She heard that Skank had stood on the Market Cross and cried out for help and that nobody came. She had held herself entirely responsible. Had she not posted her views on Skank on the town website none of this would have happened. Someone would have helped. Shifty and Skank had been in some sense lynched by her own hand. Over a period of a year she became morose and isolated. After six months she picked up a drink. And then another, and another. Because for people like Brenda, one was too many and a thousand not enough. She lost her job. She lost her home. She alienated her friends with her insistent misery and catastrophic descent in to alcohol psychosis. Her teeth fell out and she stopped dyeing her hair and washing. She became that which she had fought so hard not to be, the warty drunk old woman in the corner of the pub, spitting her teeth out in her beer and shouting "You're all bast**ds" And one night, a year and a day after she had spoken to Skank, she found herself sat in an alley in town in a pool of her own urine, shaking, hallucinating and in dire need of a drink without a penny in her purse. She had had several alcoholic fits in the last few months and could sense that one would come on in the next few hours were she not to get some alcohol inside her. The autumn night was chill and she had left her coat in the woods. She sat and rocked and shivered and prayed to anything that might save her. "Excuse me, but are you alright?" Brenda looked up. A young woman stood silhouetted against the street light. "Can I help you?" Brenda squinted. The voice was somehow familiar. She focussed harder. It was Skank. Skank looked very different. As she moved the light caught her eyes and shone on her clear skin. She was well dressed and had put on weight. She had cute shoes and the same beautiful hair cut in a shorter style. She looked concerned. She clearly didn't remember Brenda, which was unsurprising considering Brenda's dramatic decline. "What do you need?" Asked Skank "I need a drink" said Brenda. Skank knew enough drinkers, drunk and sober, to believe that this was probably the case. She put her hand in her pocket, pulled out a two pound coin and gave it to Brenda. "Here you go," she said "get some alcohol down you." Then, as an afterthought, she pulled from her other pocket a leaflet. "You might not want this," she said "but these people really helped me." Brenda took the leaflet and put it in her pocket without a glance. She was already getting to her feet in order to get to the off licence as quickly as possible. "I've had problems myself," said Skank "I know how it feels. Someone told me I needed courage and determination once. I hope you can find some of that. Do try and get some help. I'll tell you what..." she produced a pen and a piece of paper and wrote down two numbers "this is my number and this is Gracie my landlady's landline. Do give me a call if you ever need to talk."

Brenda looked Skank in the eye with an intense stare. One day she would take Skank up on her offer and beg for her forgiveness but that was not a conversation for today. "Thank you," she said, and then, as Skank turned to go, "and just one thing, what is your name?"

"My name is Hope" said the girl, as she smiled and walked away.

Other Things

Corporate Warrior

Empathieves; *my first sonnet*

Dry New World

Psychopomps

stilton

Geek Magician; *in which I have to take my computer to Currys on the bus*

Strange Poets; *for National Poetry Day*

Sip the Flip

Moving in Mysterious Ways; the All Blacks

flickering cloud; a tanka

WSMS; *my leaving poem (for all the lovely people still doing a brilliant job)*

fly by

Doorway Dogs; *for Doorway*

Bar Humbug; *my mate Ian Diddams does a reading of 'A Rugby Carol' at The Vaults, and I read this*

acton

Billy No Mates Magpie

The Mourning After The Night Before

Corporate Warrior

The concrete odour of the city clothes him
Hard shiny man, well cut of suit, and strong
With chiselled jaw grim set, close shaven
Stone cold steel in his eye, expensive
Briefcase neatly ordered, files, spreadsheets
Parker pen and plans, unfinished business
Bullet pointed, paper clipped, prioritised
Caffeine sharpened, cufflinked and unblinking
Urban warrior, an alpha male armed
For corporate war and marching for the train

Inside his heart warmed silken pocket hides
A love note and a photo of a child

Empathieves

Are empaths thieves, of feelings not their own?
Like magpies stealing precious shining rings,
They see the pain by strangers' faces shown
And understand our secret hidden things
Our tears run down their faces, our delight
May swell their hearts with love or blood or pride,
Fond friends, or someone lonely in the night
Who saw us on the telly and who cried
Unwitting thieves perhaps, but nonetheless
Possessed of power to bless or else to curse,
They know our soul while others merely guess,
May mean well and may love us much; far worse
The psychopath, who sees us without feeling,
Devoid of empathy, beyond all healing

Dry New World

When I drank
The world
Was in
My head

Now I don't drink
I'm in
The world
Instead

Psychopomps

In the eye's corner

Fluttering in photographs

Psychopomps gather

Watching for the autumn's fall

Listening to poetry

stilton; a haiku

fading summer flush

growing old with blue veined grace

an ageing stilton

Geek Magician

Techy kid, techy kid

I just don't get what you just did

I did the alt delete thing, then

I switched it off and on again

Left it alone and walked away

Had coffee and knelt down to pray

Asked nicely through my tears with love

And then repeated the above

Then went to bed and slept on it

And woke to find it still was shit

Where coloured light and words had been

Just me, reflected in the screen

No choice then but to get the bus

And beg for help, with tears and fuss

You were unassuming, cool

You watched me weep a salty pool

And kindly smiled and flicked a switch

Reducing trauma to a glitch

With just a single finger press

You saved a damsel from distress

And then you gave me good advice

Your patience was refreshing, nice

I just don't get what you just did

Or where you have your powers hid

Kids like you I shunned at school

I thought you boring and uncool

(Being) On the internet all day

Not going out to drink and play

Not trying to be hard or hot

Not caring if you are or not

But you, my friend, have kindly eyes

And keep your wisdom for the wise

You just don't need to make a show

Still waters deep with quiet flow

Techy kid, techy kid

I'm so impressed with what you did

Kind scientist and statistician

Spelling logic geek magician

Strange Poets

strange poets never cease but to amaze

with words describing things we had forgot

or never knew to start with; who knows what

may move another poet's muse to phrase

the simply indescribable in rhyme

within a string of sentences enshrine

the essence of complexity sublime

with every word a jewel within a line

strange poets see things hidden in the light

and force the formless mist within to matter

express the indefinable and flatter

dead love to life and nothingness to sight;

by use of sense and symbol and the will

they stir to movement that which once was still

Sip the Flip

I drink because I am depressed

Mate, pour yourself a thought to think

And sip on it throughout the day

Did daylight always turn to grey

Is joy within an ice cube chink

Since when was love so far away

So near the edge of some dark brink

Your tears wet your quivered lip

It's your life, who am I to say

That grief is in that glass you sip

So wet with tears you've lost your grip

Stop weeping for the missing link

And look at it a different way

I'll pour you this thought, if I may

Could it be, Mate, do you think

That you're depressed

Because you drink?

Moving in Mysterious Ways; the All Blacks

The All Blacks, man, are they for real?
They're faster than the speed of light
Don't blink, you'll miss them, they're surreal
I'm awake, not dreaming, right?
They just left the French for dead
They're faster than the speed of sound
Eyes in the back of every head
Feet that fly above the ground
What power, what fitness, what on earth
Possesses men to be that fine
What strange goddess gave them birth
What discipline keeps them in line
I sit here gobsmacked, oh my days
I understand now, here's the crack;
The All Blacks move in mysterious ways
And God plays rugby, dressed in black

flickering cloud; a tanka

fluttered by autumn

the leaves of my window tree

gave up summer's ghost

and in one flickering cloud

fell simultaneously

WSMS

Oh WSMS rhymes with bosoms
And I'm making a clean breast
I won't have a pot to piss in
So I'll give an oral test

I left my phone in Melksham
And my hamster's died, again
Forget the bloody paperwork
I've got to score in ten

It's been so high intensity
A rollercoaster ride
Times when I've been flying high
Times when I've crashed and cried

What do you mean, it's Tuesday
Your letter never came
Thanks to you I've jacked up curry
And it's starting to inflame

I'm going to miss the group work
The illicit one to one
The biscuits in the kitchen
And the friendship and the fun

My kids are starving 'cos of you
I curse you with their cries
You want me there at noon, no chance
I'll have to score some pies

You have blessed me with your wisdom
And your knowledge and your grace
I'll remember every kindly word
And every cheeky face

You don't effing understand me
You're just so middle class
Look at me that way again
I'll have you on your arse

They say for every door that closes
There's another one ajar
I'll be in a Doorway down the road
I'm so not going far

Why can't you open up at midnight
Get a doctor in for me
Because aliens took my methadone
I saw them, honestly

WSMS staff are just the business
So, with a tear in my eye
I doff my many hats to you
You're better men than I

You got me in to rehab
You wrote that important letter
You held me in the light for months
And now I'm getting better

Oh WSMS rhymes with bosoms
And I'm feeling quite a tit
Because I've gone and left out all the stuff
About it being shit

fly by; a tanka

past the lay by fly

cars with petrol in their tanks

going home for tea

we're not going anywhere

pancake flattened battery

Doorway Dogs

Winter is coming, there's frost on the ground
It's hard being homeless when you're a hound
Cold tongues and noses, wet coats and feet
Are par for the course for a dog on the street
Furry surfers of sofas and seekers of sheds
Who dream of warm fires and comfortable beds
Who can't go to the Council or bid for a flat
Who have to rely on a human for that
All that waiting outside; all that watching of doors
All that catching a wink on unsuitable floors
Living a life dodging different dangers
Living on luck and the kindness of strangers
It's a dog's life alright, and for humans as hard
It's no good in the hood when you ain't got a yard
But there's rumours afoot in the Chippenham air
Re: temporary housing and bed space to spare
Tales are wagging and shaggy dogs telling
The news that they sense on the air they are smelling
They go down to Doorway and find out it's true
"Hey doggies, we've got comfy kennels for you!"
One has a sniff and the other a lick
And one gives the new pop up kennels some stick
One crawls inside and another freaks out
"What on earth," say the dogs, "is the tent thing about?
It's hard to assimilate cultural change
The kennels, let's face it, are awfully strange
But the humans look happy and that's pretty neat
Always a good thing to keep humans sweet
And it's really quite nice of them, thinking of us
Best use the things so they don't make a fuss
Just crawl in and smile "Hey, this is quite cool!"
"Speak for yourself, mate, I feel like a tool"
"But it's warmer in here, so maybe chill out?"
"Less of the 'chill', it's the heat I'm about"

So went the debate, it was fairly immense

Till all dogs agreed that some stuff was intense

That the kennels were handy and kept out the cold

And that humans are weird and like, comedy gold

They were really quite glad that the kennels had popped up

That their core body temperatures had been topped up

And that folk gave them snacks and stuff for their dinner

Yep, the whole kennel thing was an actual winner

But lunchtime passed quickly and soon it was gone

It was time for the dogs to pack up and crack on

With doggy bags sorted they left with their folk

And went hunting for dog ends to roll up and smoke

Oh, housing's a nightmare and tricky to handle

A difficult issue, an absolute scandal

But on Mondays and Thursdays the doggies can glamp

Pop up to the drop in and hang out and camp..

In between times the Doorway staff find with a frown

That what can pop up does not always pop down

The kennels are springy and just won't play ball

And no-one can pack up the buggers at all

Goodness knows where we can stash 'em or stick 'em

Not one of us knows how to fold up and lick 'em

It's like playing Twister, such weird convolutions

Like trying to find flippin' housing solutions

Bar Humbug

Mortimer Cheese wasn't easily pleased
And he didn't like Christmas at all
At the pub where he went for his grub and a vent
He would sometimes just rant at the wall
Particularly riled by people who smiled
He would give them a piece of his mind
He just didn't get to where he was today
By being in any way kind
"Happy Christmas" they said, to the back of his head
"I think not" he would say as he turned
"Are you taking the piss?" he would splutter and hiss
Spraying mist from the beer he had earned
"Don't give me that, about Christmas, you twat
All that tinsel and plastic and light
Santa" he said, "is a paedo in red
And I'm wishing for cloud on the night
As for the star and the kings from afar
I'm for Dawkins and none of that tosh
Jesus!" he said, "You are well off your head
Bring on the shagging and nosh!"
Seven pints supped, he was just warming up
He had a few choice things to say
Some thought he joked with the words that he spoke
But most folk just melted away
One girl held a candle, despite all his scandal
They had once had a 'thing' in his car
In a zebra striped dress which she wore to impress
She watched him with lust from the bar
"Leave me off your list" he said, getting more pissed
"Not you love, I'll come in your stocking
A quick in and out, that's what Santa's about"
And other things frankly more shocking

His blood pressure rose as the atmosphere froze

And his words chilled the air of The Vaults

It seemed a good crack to stay on the attack

So he started on everyone's faults

The sad and the chubby, the hapless, the grubby

All punters were grist to his mill

"What's wrong with you folk, can you not take a joke

You're all bloody ugly or ill"

By quarter to nine he had well crossed a line

Malc the landlord said "Cheese Boy, you're barred"

"More feckin' drink" said the drunk man, "I think

That I'm better than you and well hard"

"No, you've had enough" said the landlord, "so tough

It's time you went home to your bed

You've been nasty and loud, you've done Britain First proud

And you've told us we're better off dead"

Mortimer grumbled, and stood up and stumbled

And pointed himself at the door

Knocking the bar so the big humbug jar

Fell off and smashed on the floor

"Humbugs for me" he said, grinning with glee

As he picked out a few from the glass

"I'm already sweet but these humbugs are neat"

So he necked three, and fell on his arse

"He looks a bit red" one kind punter said

"Take no notice" said someone, "he's joking"

"Stop larking about and get the f*ck out!

Oh bollocks, he's actually choking"

"Call for the Doc!" "But he called me a cock"

"Well call for the nurse then!" "She's pissed"

There was nobody there who had much of a care

There were only the folk he had dissed

A bloke at the bar, who'd been quiet so far

Who had hoped to escape any drama

Had listened to Cheese, with his bile and sleaze

And had pondered the workings of karma

Understated but cool, the bloke jumped off his stool
Someone whispered "A nice little mover"
He grabbed hold of Cheese and with confident ease
Did a swift nifty Heimlich's Manoeuvre
A grunt and a shout and the humbug shot out
Made a ring like a bell on the bar
"I'm guessing that's time then" our Mortimer said
"I'd best get me coat then, ta-ra"

As he swayed up the street he heard following feet
And a voice that was eager to please
The girl from the pub, who was stripey and sweet
"Bar Humbug" said Mortimer Cheese

acton; a tanka

parakeet flashing

pigeon perch precarious

windy acton trees

apocalyptic rumour

in the rumble of a train

Billy No Mates Magpie; My Tree

Outside my kitchen window stands a single hopeful tree

Such beauty in the ghetto is a saving grace for me

In the spring at night it's silver buds shine like tiny stars

Twinkling by the bin store and the white vans and the cars

In summer green it's vibrant leaves shade cat dirt covered grass

And flicker subtle shadows on my kitchen window glass

In the autumn there are berries, for tiny birds to eat

Glowing brighter than the sunset, falling red on grimy street

So many contemplative pigeons seeking sanctuary I've seen

So many blue tits, sparrows, robins, adding colours to the green

Squirrels, blackbirds, starlings; quarrels, lovemaking and chat

The cuckoo of a carrier bag, the stranded curious cat

One day they will chop it down and all that will be left

Will be the tarmac and the garages, and I shall be bereft

In the meantime, it is winter; naked branches cold and bare

And a single lonely magpie, every morning, sitting there

Usually with magpies, if you wait a little time

Another bird will come, to bring you joy, as in the rhyme

I watch the skies with hopeful eyes from early dawn till late

Can he be the only magpie in the world without a mate

The magpie sits alone and waits, he'll be alone tomorrow

Billy No Mates Magpie

And his sorrow

The Mourning After the Year Before

"Knock, knock" "Who's there?" I haven't a clue
What day is it? Who's at my door?
"Here is some breakfast I made just for you"
Says some stranger who slept on my floor
The sight of the eggs and the bacon and tea
Turns my stomach inside upside down
Migraine's the price that I've paid for the glee
Of a banging night out on the town
"'Ere, it's New Year, do you fancy a beer?"
"No thanks, mate, I'm feeling quite rough"
I may have blacked out after midnight I fear
But now I'm...remembering...Stuff
Slowly but surely it's coming to mind
As glimpses emerge from the fog
Of a twist and a twerk and a bump and a grind
And my new Christmas phone down the bog
I thought I was hot but in retrospect not
In the morning light nowt could be plainer
And that I remember I like not a jot
My naked and drunk Macarena
Oh me and my mates, we do get in a state
And last year we gave it some welly
But if anyone had not enough on their plate
We'd do onesies and pizza and telly
My mates are my life, we're a pretty tight bunch
They're alright, mate, they're really all right
But last night I must have been well out to lunch
For I reckon I started a fight...
It was something to do with a girl I once knew
And a joke that she did stuff for money
And a fine upper cut in the queue for the loo
Well, I thought the punch line was funny
Oh, what's in my pockets, this isn't my coat
As I'm clearly not Super or Dry

And what are the words that are writ on this note

'Bell me, baby, you're totally fly'

And I'm going commando, hilarious bants

Will be had in regards to my loss

Much mirth to be had from the sight of my pants

On the top of the Market Cross

It's not looking good, and tucked in to my hood

Are two gherkins all wrapped in a bra

Half a kebab and a squashed Christmas pud

And a wing mirror nicked from a car

I think I'm experiencing chemical guilt

And at some point I'll have to atone

But right now I'm going to hide under my quilt

Crying blubbery tears for my phone

Christians, Druids, and Light

God Loves Little Jacqui Clark; *for the Reverend Jacqui Clark*

Sad Insanity

Demeter's Lament; *written for the Autumn Equinox and the Gorsedd of the Bards at Avebury*

Obscure Bloom; the Eclipse

Darkness Becoming Visible; November

Angelic Imperfection

Harriet's Gift; *for Harriet Lane*

The Solstice Door; *for the Winter Solstice, and the Gorsedd*

Midnight Mass; St. John's

The Curious Offering of the Sacristan

Let Me In

Well, Well, Welby; *the Archbishop of Canterbury says that it is not racist to query immigration*

The Angel of the North; *I weep at the feet of the Angel of the North*

Strange Simony

She Comes; *for the Spring Equinox, and the Gorsedd*

Granny's Easter Buns

The Veil of the Temple

Justin Welby's Dad

Suddenly

God loves little Jacqui Clark

God loves little Jacqui Clark
With all her kind and merry ways
Bright darling candle in the dark
Dear joyful soul who lights our days
Thank you, Jacqui, for the love
You bear to heal our hurt and pain
For blesséd manna from above
Flows forth from you
Like gentle rain

Sad Insanity

the eye remembers

bright shadows of dying suns

invisible light

wild spring lust faded

satiated summer sleep

restless autumn dreams

there will be winter

endless overwhelming night

inevitable

knowledge of the tides

may save the soul from drowning

sad insanity

Demeter's Lament

abandoned flowers, empty field
three strands of hair lit rose and gold
last ray of sun caught by my shield
I, Demeter, am growing old

upon the ground an aspen wreath
rustles faintly in the breeze
for she is gone to worlds beneath
the falling leaves and dying trees

horizons kissed by half a sun
in perfect balance, day and night
lost is my child, my precious one
to darkness, hidden from my sight

gathered harvest, winter store
remembered heat, descending cold
the closing of an open door
and tales of her beauty told

grapes plucked from the writhing vine
made sacred wine before she left
how I miss thee, daughter mine
now I am Demeter, bereft

hear your mother mourn for thee
and call your name through falling tears
return, my daughter, come to me
when green shoots rise and life appears

so many moons will wax and wane
as for my child I keen and moan
no hope of spring will soothe my pain
for I am Demeter, alone

when we meet again, my child
you will no more a maiden be
changed by the underworld, beguiled
this, I Demeter, will see

this winter I become a crone
and fade and dry like a funeral wreath
the lines on my face by sorrow grown
Demeter, consumed by grief

my feet fall where her foot fall fell
to the sound of the green man's laughing glee
and I find myself at the gate of hell
weeping for my Persephone

'twas ever thus, no less the pain
the sun goes down, the sun comes up
there shall be wine and joy again
I, Demeter, will share that cup

the wings of a whistling swan in flight
cast shadows of light upon the water
will you wait with me at the gate of night
for my beloved, my daughter

Obscure Bloom; the Eclipse

Obscuring the moon
A veil of rose and ashes
Fades and overwhelms

Memory of light
Lost imprint of blossom bloom
Imperceptible

Through black spaces move
Things unearthly and unseen
Stirring the shadows

Earth falls to silence
Darkness comprehending not
What may yet become

Darkness becoming Visible; November

Within a pumpkin's hollow is a candle burning bright

We have prayed the dead to silence, we have sent them to the light

Bring in dark November, let the winter cold begin

Stick the heating on and let the Saints come marching in

There will be icy dawns and fireworks, dank leaves and naked trees

We shall wish for Christmas jumpers to protect against the freeze

Is it colder now than last year? Oh, where did the year go

By the time we've got a grip we will be sliding in the snow

We will remember that November gives birth to the Advent season

And that once the knives were out for Fawkes for gunpowder and treason

We shall wish for bonfires high enough to chase the night away

As we watch the winter shadows fill the corners of the day

We have been tricked, we have been cheated; now it's all downhill from here

Until we come to rest, at Christmas, when a new light will appear

Angelic Imperfection

Late for the Nativity

I stand among the throng

Self-consciously

Singing with the angels

Quietly

Sensing the future

Yearning out

In front of me

Revealed

Symbolically

How it will

Always be

Odd one out

For all to see

The only angel

Without wings

Harriet's Gift

Today, my dear friend Harriet gave to me
A tiny glittery nativity
Like Russian dolls, the size of half a thumb
A tiny Joseph Dad and Mary Mum
And Jesus, smaller than a fingernail
Such tiny things to tell so grand a tale
And as she pressed them in my hand her eyes
So bright and hopeful, old and kind and wise
Were simply brimming with that shining light
That fuelled the star that lit that mystic night
Some weeks ago, she gifted me a stone
Found on a beach where she had walked alone
All gold and smooth from rolling ocean's wear
For me to hold in moments of despair
And there were candles then, that she had lit
Upon the table where we sometimes sit
And then, like now, I very nearly cried
So touched by all the love she has inside
If only love and Christmas were like this
All simple joy, delight and friendly kiss
All gentleness, all light and subtle sheen
Like all the things in her that I have seen
I wish you joy, like Harriet wishes me
A Christmas full of love; all blessèd be

The Solstice Door

Behind the running, running man the land
Lies silent, fallow, haunted by the cry
Of one lone mourning rook who flies alone
Inscribing solemn circles in the sky
There is no time to take a backward look
Just running, running, running, running blind
He leaves the flowered garlands that she wove
With ribbons bright, with summer's love, behind
He runs with only hope in empty hands
All faint of heart, with life blood running cold
The chill of winter earth beneath his feet
All water turned to ice in frozen fold
All out of breath with minutes yet to live
He runs, through elder grove and stand of yew
Runs, seeking for the ancient Solstice door
Described in tales the bards and ancients knew
'Till suddenly he stumbles on a glade
All silent where no wild bird wheels or calls
And in the glade there stands a single stone
And on the ground a moon dark shadow falls
And there, within the shadow's light he sees
That which before him other men have found
A stairway leading down in to the earth
A dark descending path in to the ground
No way but down now, this the only way
He gathers one last breath, and full of fear
Goes down the old and foot worn ancient steps
That lead towards the portal of the year
How dark the endless steps of winter's stair
That shadow down, down to the Solstice door
To where, beneath the door a chink of light
Hints soft and bright across the cold stone floor
He sits upon the bottom step to rest
Reflect, and contemplate the year behind

And lo, she comes, bedecked in leaves and fruit

And dancing, dancing, through his weary mind

Forget me not, she sings; I am still here

I wait for you, for life to shift and stir

And through the keyhole and the chink there blows

A fragrant waft of birch and silver fir

Reviving, blessing, soft upon his face

The promise of new life upon her breath

Touched by her grace he weeps upon the step

For she has saved him with her love from death

Another year dies, another lives

He sits and waits; she watches from afar

And as he waits the light in darkness shifts

And creaks the ancient Solstice Door ajar...

Midnight Mass; St. John's

Church on Christmas Eve
Experience of spirit
Secular delight

Candles flickering
Stirred by one communal breath
Casting bright shadows

The choir whispering
Mournful cadenced melodies
That bless the silence

Drunken folk giggling
Respectfully hiccupping
Noisy chundering

Strange and precious faith
The uninitiated
Wary, questioning

Through agnostic eyes
Such peculiar mystery
Custom, novelty

The truth hides in love
Ancient priests and children know
It's simplicity

The door is opened
Out in to the night The Word
Flies on sacred wings

Midnight Mass; the light

In darkness comprehending

Emptiness with joy

The Curious Offering of the Sacristan

The curious offerings of sacristans
Are given in obscure humility
The symbol of the cupping of the hands
Enshrines the essence of this mystery
The dawn unlocked; the turning of a key
The mystic world behind the little door
The mourning weepers, watching, silently
The quiet foot upon uneven floor
The layered shadowed centuries; the pass
Of long dead worshippers before the throne
Slow shifts of coloured pools of stains of glass
Soft drift of latticed light on pillar stone
The empty candle, thirsting for new oil
Unscrewed and filled, screwed up again and lit
The hidden corners, carved by masons' toil
In which a wary flickered flame may flit
The covering, uncovering; each fold
Of linen and of altar cloth an art
Within the starch of white, on marble cold
The space to hold His living, beating heart
Here, understated wafers wait in line
For blessing, as an unblessed congregation
Here silver, water, light, and red wine shine
Anticipating sacred consecration
Here eye, and hand, and mind, seek symmetry
In objects placed, in psychic ebbs and flows
Seek that perfection only God can see
In right angle and scented mystic rose
When all are done and gone, her hands will shake
The fragments of His flesh on holy ground
Shed drops upon the earth its thirst to slake
Pour water through the light without a sound
When all are gone, all blessed with wine and bread
There, in the East, where better men have trod

She kneels and presses to the step her head

And, lost in awe, she speaks these words to God

I am that ancient soul you always knew

A part of you, from when time first began

The I am that I am, the that in you

That serves thee, as I will, while still I can

I come to you as Christian, Muslim, Jew

Agnostic, Gnostic, Druid, Angel, Man

The cupping of my hands I give to you

The curious offering of a sacristan

Let Me In

Knock, knock, who's there, and art thou friend or foe?
Why knockest thou at this ungodly hour?
I am the Light, whose face and word you know
I bring you sheaves of blossom trees in flower
So many moons have passed since we last met
How shall I know that it is really you?
I am the Light no darkness can forget
I bring you skies of bright and endless blue
Why comest thou, now I am nearly old
With fainting faith and blood flow slow and dry?
I am the Light, returning as foretold
I bring you Life, to raise you true and high
How glad am I, to see you at my door
Come, cast your crazy sunbeams on my floor

Well, Well, Welby

Well, well, Welby
Beg your pardon
He's got three Poles
At the bottom of his garden
And joining in with daily prayers
Some Syrians, beneath the stairs
Asylum seekers in his shed
And Communists
Beneath his bed

He's just doing what he can
To pander to the 'common' man
To separate the issues, see
Of race, and the economy
With good intent, to bridge the gap
'Twixt logic and the racist crap
For Welby is a diplomat
Just in case, and just like that

It's not that we're a racist state
Good luck with that one, Welby, mate
Imagine pubs across the land
The dodgy banter, beer in hand
That Archbishop got it right
We're all white mate, we're all white
Share our wealth with all the planet?
Outrageous! (outraged Bob from Thanet)

But what of all the fish and bread
With which five thousand mouths were fed
Would Jesus Christ have found it hard
To put up Poles in his back yard?

The Angel of the North

Another bloody southerner
Shedding tears at my steely feet
I stand in judgement over you
See me and weep

Tell the angels of the south
To bless you with their feathered sympathy
I have no eyes to cry for you
Nor close in sleep

This is my body, glorious
Within my breast a thousand hammers beat
I cast a shadow over you
See me and weep

Strange Simony

Another man

Another plan

Hung on a

Godforsaken tree

One dread kiss

And then

Was this

Eternal calumny

How bitter

Seems the glitter

Of dark silver

Simony

No shining glory

In this story

Just shame and death

For all to see

In the daylight

And with hindsight

Could not there

Light and mercy be

For it was writ

This would be it

That all these things

Would come to be

The portrayal

Of his betrayal

Haunts our own

Humanity

No kudos

For poor Judas

Only lonely

Ignominy

She Comes; a Rhyme for the Spring Equinox

For all the night she trod the furrowed earth
As she has walked all winter in her wake
In seeking for the child she brought to birth
The maiden bride whom Hades chose to take

The gibbous moon is waxing to the bright
And shedding shifting shadows on the lands
One single moonbeam spills down through the night
Upon the rutted earth on which she stands

Made heavy by the weight of mother's tears
The ground beneath her feet begins to yield
The imprint of a child's foot appears
Emerging from the darkness of the field

The dawn is tinting grey the silken skies
The lifting mist moves gulls to take the air
She swears she hears these words within their cries
She comes, she comes, she comes, is nearly there...

Around the hill of Silbury swirl the springs
From many sources meeting there as one
Upon the fence a bardic blackbird sings
His songs of seasons ended and begun

The heron stands in wait down by the brook
The willows' leaves weave rills upon the stream
The cormorant is fishing for the rook
Whose shadow shapes a fish from daybreak's gleam

From alder trees drip drops of ancient dew
Like shining crystals, in to waters deep
The grey of morn becomes a brighter blue
New lambs are woken from the dark womb's sleep

A muffled drumbeat pounds within her bones
Thrills through her feet and trembles in her chest
Draws from four corners people of the stones
To stand and lay the winter to his rest

Can it be so, she thinks, that she will come
And willingly escape the thrall of Hades
Be called by this fast beating of the drum
To dance among the wild lords-and-ladies

The drum, the drum, the Druid in the East
The daylight shattering the glass of night
Behold the mead and cake that form the feast
Behold the glorious blessing of the light

The blazing gorse flames yellow on the hill
Bright shafts of sun surround the Druid's head
She comes, she comes, my daughter liveth still
Released at last from fathoms of the dead

Her eyes are purple crocuses, her hair
Is woven through with wood anemones
She shocks the eyes, her presence is so rare
And strong, as hyacinths upon the breeze

She wears the sun a-shimmer on her dress
In folds of drops of snow and celandines
And, as befits she with the power to bless
Comes riding on a stag of seven tines

She speaks unto the awed and silent crowd
"I come" she says "I bring the fire of life
I come to cast my seeds on fields ploughed
To quell your hunger and relieve your strife

I bring you daylight from the depths of hell
Where I with Hades am forever wed
Of Christ and Dionysus I shall tell
In sacred stories of the risen dead"

The crowd are stunned to silence, robbed of breath
She came, she came, brought winter to his knees
Defied the dreadful tide of dark and death
To bless the ground with shoots, and trees with leaves

The ancient Druid offers up the cup
The wine of her libations there to sip
He bows his head, as down she stoops to sup
And touch the cup upon her rosy lip

And with this act the sunlight floods the sky
The spell is broken by the touch of earth
And Demeter runs forward with a cry
To hold the maiden that she brought to birth

The seasons come, the seasons go, and all
Shall rise and fall and fade and reappear
And Spring shall once more answer to the call
Of Hades at the dying of the year

But here, by mother love and heat of day
Persephone is made a child again
To run upon the hills; to dance and play
And plant her flowers in the world of men

Granny's Easter Buns

Grandad says that Easter isn't funny
You won't find him at parties
Dressed up as the Easter bunny
He'll not be scoffing chocolate eggs
Or anything like that
He'll be putting on his Sunday best
And dusting off his hat
For Grandad is an Anglican
Of serious intent
Does bible study when he can
And gave up cake for Lent
He says that Jesus died for me
And I'd best not forget it
But seeing as I'm only three
I'm sorry, I don't get it
My Granny, now my Granny, mind
She has a different view
She leaves me little eggs to find
In places like my shoe
The smell of Granny's hot cross buns
Is paradise and bliss
She makes me little special ones
Topped with a tiny kiss
Granny says God loves me
As she makes my Easter bonnet
With a smile as she carefully
Sews flowers and bees upon it
Let Grandad do religious stuff
The crucifixion thing
I'm only really old enough
For Granny, and the Spring

Grandad's back from church now

Saying 'Jesus rose for you'

'Well, bless us all' my Granny says

'The buns are risen too'

The Veil of the Temple

The veil of the temple is

Rent from above

And all that is left

On the altar is

Love

Justin Welby's Dad

Poor old Justin Welby

It must have been a shock

To find out that he issued from

Churchill's PA's cock

Not from the Holy Spirit

Or the fairies after all

Not a babe in a basket under a bush

Down by the garden wall

It was a diplomatic missive

That brought about his seeding

Four dots dash dot dot dash, it said

Destroy this after reading

For poor old Mother Welby

It was just a drunken shag

But Browne had an Archbishop

In his diplomatic bag

And, he really was quite dashing

With his huge unholy boner

You would though, wouldn't you, so

Let the sinless queue to stone her

Welby ponders wisely

Prays, and has a cup of tea

Questions divine purposes

And how he came to be

And comes to the conclusion

That it matters not a jot

As long as there are biscuits

And his tea is piping hot

For this is Christianity

And though it may seem odd

In the game of 'Who's yer Father'

Justin Welby's Dad is God

Suddenly

The dead go down violently, suddenly, silently

Down in the drown of the deep

The born rise up hopefully, suddenly, quietly

Rise from the depths of their sleep

The night will fall dreadfully, suddenly, softly

Fall on the land in a heap

The day shall jump joyfully, suddenly, gently

Jump with a quickening leap

Let the darkness dawn mournfully, suddenly, slowly

Dark on the flood and the seep

For the light shineth endlessly, suddenly, subtly

Bright on the rivers we weep

About the Author

Gail Foster was born in Bath, and lives in Devizes in Wiltshire, England.

She writes, and takes commissions

takes photographs, makes images and performs poetry, as

Gail from Devizes